# ALDOUS HUXLEY

\*

*Do What You Will*

# By ALDOUS HUXLEY

### Novels
CROME YELLOW *
ANTIC HAY *
THOSE BARREN LEAVES *
POINT COUNTER POINT *
BRAVE NEW WORLD *
EYELESS IN GAZA *
AFTER MANY A SUMMER *
TIME MUST HAVE A STOP
APE AND ESSENCE

### Short Stories
LIMBO *
MORTAL COILS *
LITTLE MEXICAN *
TWO OR THREE GRACES *
BRIEF CANDLES *

### Biography
GREY EMINENCE

### Essays and Belles Lettres
ON THE MARGIN *
ALONG THE ROAD *
PROPER STUDIES *
DO WHAT YOU WILL *
MUSIC AT NIGHT & *
VULGARITY IN LITERATURE
TEXTS AND PRETEXTS (Anthology) *
THE OLIVE TREE *
ENDS AND MEANS (An Enquiry
into the Nature of Ideals) *
THE ART OF SEEING
THE PERENNIAL PHILOSOPHY
SCIENCE, LIBERTY AND PEACE

### Travel
JESTING PILATE (Illustrated) *
BEYOND THE MEXIQUE BAY (Illustrated) *

### Poetry and Drama
VERSES AND A COMEDY *
(including early poems, Leda, The Cicadas
and The World of Light, a Comedy)
THE GIOCONDA SMILE

*Issued in this Collected Edition

ALDOUS HUXLEY

# Do What You Will

*Twelve Essays*

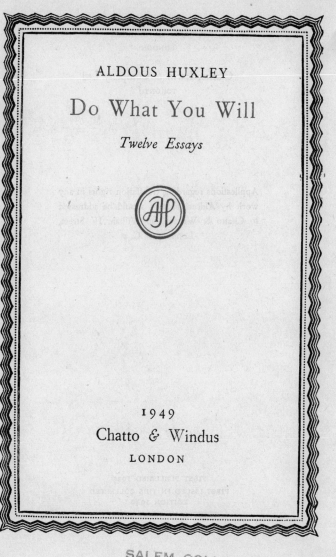

1949

Chatto & Windus

LONDON

PUBLISHED BY

Chatto & Windus

LONDON

✳

Clarke, Irwin & Company Ltd

TORONTO

Applications regarding translation rights in any
work by Aldous Huxley should be addressed
to Chatto & Windus, 40 William IV Street,
London, W.C. 2

FIRST PUBLISHED 1929
FIRST ISSUED IN THIS COLLECTED
EDITION 1949
PRINTED IN GREAT BRITAIN

# CONTENTS

# DO WHAT YOU WILL

## ONE AND MANY

### § 1. *Introduction*

There are many kinds of Gods. Therefore there are many kinds of men. For men make Gods in their own likeness. To talk about religion except in terms of human psychology is an irrelevance. ' Aphrodite, you say, came with my son to Menelaus' house.' It is Hecuba who speaks, in Euripides's *Trojan Women*, to the disastrous Helen. ' How laughable ! . . . When you saw him it was your own thought that became Aphrodite. Aphrodite is the name for every human folly.' And similarly Jehovah, Allah, the Trinity, Jesus, Buddha are names for a great variety of human virtues, human mystical experiences, human aesthetic emotions, human remorses, human compensatory fancies, human terrors, human cruelties. If all men were alike, all the world would worship the same God. Aphrodite, however, bears little resemblance to Calvin's Jehovah, Siva is singularly unlike the Something not ourselves that makes for the righteousness of cultured modernists. *Quot homines, tot dei.*

Even the same man is not consistently the worshipper of one God. Officially an agnostic, I *feel* the presence of devils in a tropical forest.

Confronted, when the weather is fine and I am
in propitious emotional circumstances, with certain landscapes, certain works of art, certain
human beings, I *know*, for the time being, that
God's in his heaven and all's right with the
world. On other occasions, skies and destiny
being inclement, I am no less immediately
certain of the malignant impersonality of an
uncaring universe. Every human being has had
similar experiences. This being so, the sensible
thing to do would be to accept the facts and frame
a metaphysic to fit them. But with that talent
for doing the wrong thing, that genius for perversity, so characteristically human, men have
preferred, especially in recent times, to take
another course. They have either denied the
existence of these psychological facts ; or if they
have admitted them, have done so only to condemn as evil all such experiences as cannot be
reconciled in a logical system with whatever
particular class of experiences they have chosen,
arbitrarily, to regard as ' true ' and morally
valuable. Every man tries to pretend that he
is consistently one kind of person, and does
his best consistently to worship one kind of
God. And this despite the fact that he experiences diversity and actually feels himself
in contact with a variety of divinities (or at
any rate with extremely dissimilar aspects of
the same Unknown God who may be presumed
to lie behind them all).

## § 2. *The Question of Truth*

The only facts of which we have direct knowledge are psychological facts. The Nature of
Things presents us with them. There is no getting round them, or behind them, or outside of
them. They are there, given.

One fact cannot be more of a fact than another.
Our psychological experiences are all equally
facts. There is nothing to choose between them.
No psychological experience is ' truer,' so far as
we are concerned, than any other. For even if
one should correspond more closely to things in
themselves as perceived by some hypothetical
non-human being, it would be impossible for us
to discover which it was. ' There never has been
and never will be a man who has certain knowledge about the Gods and about all the things I
speak of. For even if he should happen to speak
the whole truth, yet he himself does not know it ;
but all may have their fancy.' So wrote Xeno-
phanes some two thousand five hundred years
ago. In spite of which, men still continue to
promote their fancies to the rank of universal
and absolute Truths, still imagine that they know
something about the thing in itself. But the
thing in itself is unknowable and ' all may have
their fancy ' about it. Science is no ' truer ' than
common-sense or lunacy, than art or religion.
It permits us to organize our experience profit-
ably ; but tells us nothing about the real nature

of the world to which our experiences are supposed to refer. From the internal reality, by
which I mean the totality of psychological
experiences, it actually separates us. Art, for
example, deals with many more aspects of this
internal reality than does science, which confines
itself deliberately and by convention to the study
of one very limited class of experiences—the
experiences of sense. To collect records of sense
experiences (particularly of those which lend
themselves to description in terms of numbers),
to generalize them, to draw inferences from them,
to construct from them a logically harmonious
scheme of description and explanation—this is
the business of science. At the moment, it is
worth remarking, there is no scheme that harmoniously reconciles all the facts even in the
limited sphere of scientific investigation. What
is sense in the sub-atomic universe is pure nonsense in the macroscopical world. In other
words, logic compels us to draw one set of inferences from certain sense experiences and another
irreconcilable set of inferences from certain other
sense experiences.

Less loudly, indeed, than in the past and less
insistently, Science and Logic still claim, through
the mouths of their professional spokesmen, to
be able to arrive at the Truth. The claim is one
which it is hard to justify.

Take logic. Logic, it is true, enables us to
transcend immediate experience, to infer from the

4

known existence of A and B the hitherto unsuspected existence of C. In practice, however, we always try to verify experimentally the theoretical results obtained by means of logical argument. Not so much because we mistrust the logical process as because we mistrust the premisses from which the process must start. For if our premisses do not correspond with reality, the conclusions, though obtained by logically faultless deduction, will also fail to correspond with reality. It is always difficult to be sure that our premisses *do* correspond with reality. Hence the need to test results experimentally. The external world has proved to be surprisingly obedient to logic. When we conclude from well-chosen premisses that something must be so, it has turned out in practice to be so, ' really.' Will the world always show such deference to our laws of thought? The physicists are at present involved in such difficulties that some pessimists have suggested that the universe is fundamentally irrational. One can only shrug one's shoulders and hope for the best. Either, then, the world is irrational, and logically necessary conclusions from real premisses do not always and necessarily correspond with reality. Or else the world is rational, and conclusions drawn from real premisses must themselves be real. But the difficulty in this latter case is to be sure that the premisses do completely correspond with reality—whatever reality may be (which nobody knows)—or even with what we have chosen, for the particular purposes of the moment, to regard as reality. It is so great, that we try wherever possible to check theoretical results by experiment. And in those very numerous cases where they cannot be checked? Again, one can only shrug one's shoulders and hope for the best. The theologians have wisely insisted that faith shall supplement reason.

So much for logic. What, now, of the claims of the natural sciences, based on observation? Consider, in this connection, a chair. What sort of chair, you ask, how old and made by whom? For the sake of simplicity, and to help the poor scientist, I will ignore these questions, even though they refer to what are quite obviously the most important aspects of the chair. An oak chair made by machinery for any one of a million Babbitts is radically different from an oak chair made by a mediæval craftsman for a prince of the Church. The two chairs are different in the quality of what we are forced, for lack of better expressions, to call their souls, their characters, their forms of life. For the sake of simplicity, however, I will ignore all the aspects of the chair that every human being spontaneously feels to be the most significant, and concentrate exclusively on its ponderable and measurable aspects—on those aspects, in a word, with which science has elected to deal.

To the gross senses the chair seems solid and

substantial. But the gross senses can be refined by means of instruments. Closer observations are made, as the result of which we are forced to conclude that the chair is ' really ' a swarm of electric charges whizzing about in empty space. If it were in our power to make observations with other organs than those with which nature has endowed us, the same logic would certainly compel us to believe that the chair was ' really ' something quite unlike both the substantial object made by joiners, and sold on the instalment system, and the swarm of electric charges. All that we are finally justified in affirming is that the psychological experience called ' substantial chair ' is the one we have to rely on as ' true ' in one set of circumstances, while the experience, ' electric-charge chair,' must be regarded as ' true ' in other circumstances and for other purposes. The substantial-chair experience is felt to be intrinsically more satisfactory, because we are more accustomed to it. Our normal everyday life is passed in the midst, not of whizzing electric charges, but of substantial objects. Both types of chair are abstractions. But while the substantial chair is an abstraction easily made from the memories of innumerable sensations of sight and touch, the electric-charge chair is a difficult and far-fetched abstraction from certain visual sensations so excessively rare (they can only come to us in the course of elaborate experiments) that not one man in a million

7

has ever been in the position to make it for himself. The overwhelming majority of us accept the electric-charge chair on authority, as good Catholics accept transubstantiation. We have faith and we believe. Quite without genuine conviction. What we are genuinely convinced of is the solid substantiality of chairs. Which is ' really ' illusory.

What is the position, in the hierarchy of truths, of the individual sensations from which we abstract our substantial objects, collections of electric charges, or whatever else we care to fabricate from these elementary experiences ? In practice we are continually, and for the most part automatically, correcting our immediate sensations. This cock - eyed two - dimensional figure, of which some parts are coloured in light tones and some in dark, and which changes its shape and the disposition of its colours as we walk past it, is ' really ' a cubical box seen in perspective. This collection of irregular surfaces which I touch with my finger-tips is ' really ' a solid stone. And so on. The capacity to make such corrections is characteristically human. Animals, even the higher animals, seem to ' believe all they see.' What they see (which is more or less what we see in its primitive uncorrected state)—is it falser, in any absolute sense of the word, than that which we abstract from our immediate sensations ? Is the appearance, to use the phraseology of Plato, intrinsically and absolutely less true than the Idea ? Plato himself would have answered in the affirmative. Appearances are illusory ; Ideas (our abstractions from remembered appearances) are true. But considering the matter with a little attention, we perceive that there is no more reason why an abstraction made after the fact should be nearer to the thing in itself than an immediate sensation. It is only for certain strictly human purposes that the Idea can be considered truer than the appearance. Abstracted from a mass of the most diverse sensations, the Idea is a sort of Lowest Common Measure of appearances. For the purposes of Man the remembering and foreseeing animal, of Man the exerciser of persistent and conscious action on the external world, the Idea or abstraction is truer than the immediate sensation. It is because we are predominantly purposeful beings that we are perpetually correcting our immediate sensations. But men are free not to be utilitarianly purposeful. They can sometimes be artists, for example. In which case they may like to accept the immediate sensation uncorrected, because it happens to be beautiful. They will like the form of the cockeyed two-dimensional figure and refuse to let themselves be distracted by the thought that it is ' really ' a box. For such people the immediate sensation, or ' appearance,' will be truer than the abstraction, or ' Idea.' In any case, the criterion of truth and falsehood must always remain

internal, psychological. To talk about truth as
a relationship between human notions and things
in themselves is an absurdity.

## § 3. *Human Nature and Divine Nature*

Truth is internal. One psychological fact is
as good as another. Having established these
principles, we can now begin to talk, with some
hope of talking sensibly, about religion.

' I believe in one God,' affirms the church-
goer ; and almost any right-thinking man would
be ready, if you asked him what he believed in,
to say the same. In one God. But why not
in sixty-four Gods, or two hundred and seventeen Gods ? Because monotheism is fashionable
in twentieth-century Europe. If it were not, all
right-thinking people would obviously be affirming their belief in sixty-four or two hundred and
seventeen, or whatever other number of Gods
happened to be prescribed by the competent
authorities. One right-thinking man thinks like
all other right-thinking men of his time—that is
to say, in most cases, like some wrong-thinking
man of another time. Mr. Jones believes in one
God, because Mr. Smith believes in one God, and
incidentally, because a good many centuries ago
Plato and numerous Jews, including Jesus, believed in one God.

But why did it ever occur to any one to believe
in only one God ? And, conversely, why did it

ever occur to any one to believe in many Gods ?
To both these questions we must return the same
answer : Because that is how the human mind
happens to work. For the human mind is both
diverse and simple, simultaneously many and
one. We have an immediate perception of our
own diversity and of that of the outside world.
And at the same time we have immediate perceptions of our own oneness. Occasionally also,
in certain states which may vaguely be described
as mystical, we have an immediate perception of
an external unity, embracing and (paradoxically—
but we actually experience the paradox) embraced by our own internal unity ; we *feel* the
whole universe as a single individual mysteriously
fused with ourselves. Moreover, by a process of
abstraction, of generalization, of logical reasoning,
we can discover in the outside world a principle
of unity, none the less genuine for the fact that
we have very possibly put it there ourselves. The
sixpence I find in my Christmas pudding is still
sixpence, even though it was I who gave it to the
cook. If the world presents itself to me as a
unity as well as a diversity, that is because I myself am one as well as many. Perceiving, I create
my world, perhaps out of nothing but the stuff
of my own mind, perhaps out of things in themselves—who knows ? Fatally and necessarily,
however, I create it in my own image. If I were
wholly diverse—a mere succession in time of unconnected states—I should obviously inhabit a

wholly diverse universe, in which instant succeeded discrete instant, event followed causeless and resultless event, incoherently. If, on the contrary, I were a simple perfected unity, my world would be as simply perfect as the universe inhabited by a stone. That is to say, it would be non-existent, since I myself would have no consciousness either of my own or of any other existence. For perfection is the same as non-existence ; and, undivided against itself, uncontrasted with diversity, the One is the equivalent of the Nothing.

We are aware of existing ; therefore we are not merely one. We are conscious of remaining ourselves through inward and outward change ; therefore we are not merely diverse. Given these peculiarities of human nature, it is easy to infer the peculiarities of divine nature. Men are both simple and diverse ; therefore there are many Gods and therefore there is only one God.

History confirms a theoretical conclusion. In certain tracts of space and time, there is no God but God ; in others, the local pantheons are overcrowded like so many slum tenements. In yet others, men have made a compromise in their mythology between unity and diversity. Olympus is no more a democracy, but a monarchy ruled by an emperor who chooses to delegate certain powers to his officials. Or else the celestial drama is not acted by a stock company of divinities—it is a quick-change turn, where all the parts are played by a single performer. We see Thor and Wotan, Athena and Aphrodite, Krishna and Siva. They act convincingly, in character. But they are not really there at all. An anonymous demiurge with an extraordinary talent for male, female, and hermaphroditic impersonation simultaneously plays all their parts.

## § 4. *Progress in Mythology*

It is generally assumed that belief in one God succeeds belief in many Gods, and that this succession is in the nature of a spiritual progress. But monotheism is sometimes found, if we may believe the accounts of travellers, in the most primitive societies. Nor are all the members of one society more than nominally of one faith. This is true, as Mr. Radin, a student of Red Indian habits and customs, has pointed out, even of rigidly intolerant primitive communities. Belief in one or in many Gods is determined by the idiosyncrasies of the believer. There are born polytheists and born monotheists. There are also born neutrals, who passively accept the views of the majority or of individuals with stronger personalities than their own, and become either ' right-thinking men ' or else the ' misguided dupes ' of heresiarchs, whichever the case may be. Those in whom the unifying tendency predominates, whether in the form of a mystical gift for feeling the world's oneness, or of a talent for generalization and abstraction, worship one God. Those who are conscious predominantly of their own and the world's diversity worship many Gods.

Not only among the Red Indians, but also among those who profess and call themselves Christians, Atheists, Theosophers, Anthroposophers, Occultists, Agnostics, and so forth, we can find, as well as Nature's gentlemen and Nature's cads, her unitarians and her polytheists, her fetish-worshippers and her neo-platonists. Orthodoxies may be strict ; but the religion of any society is always extremely mixed. This is a fact which we must always and steadily bear in mind when we talk of contemporary monotheism. But even if we do bear it in mind, we are forced, I think, to admit that there has been a genuine trend in recent times towards a unitarian mythology and the worship of one God. This is the tendency which it has been customary to regard as a spiritual progress. On what grounds ? Chiefly, so far as one can see, because we in the twentieth-century West are officially the worshippers of a single divinity. A movement whose consummation is *Us* must be progressive. *Quod erat demonstrandum.*

For those, however, who dislike the present dispensation this argument will hardly seem convincing. In their eyes a movement that concludes in *Us* seems the reverse of progressive.

Almost all historical discussions, it should be

noticed, are discussions of personal tastes. Thus, both Flinders Petrie and Spengler believe in the cyclic recurrence of history. But their cycles are not the same, because their standards of civilization and barbarism, or in other words their tastes in literature, art, religion, and morals, happen to differ. Most of the arguments for and against the reality of progress are similarly oblique statements of the arguer's personal tastes. Having thus given due warning, I can now proceed to consider the question : Is the displacement of polytheism by monotheism a progress ?

## § 5. *Monotheism*

Monotheism, as we know it in the West, was invented by the Jews. These unfortunate inhabitants of the desert found nothing in the surrounding bareness to make them suppose that the world was richly diverse. It was easy for them to conceive the deity as one and disembodied. ' L'extrême simplicité de l'esprit sémitique,' says Renan, ' sans étendue, sans diversité, sans arts plastiques, sans philosophie, sans mythologie, sans vie politique, sans progrès, n'a pas d'autre cause : il n'y a pas de variété dans le monothéisme.' Conversely, he might have added, there can be no polytheism in minds by nature or by habit so sterile, so ungenerous of fruits. Except for a little literature, the Jews and Arabs produced nothing humanly valuable until they left their deserts, came into contact with the polytheistic races and absorbed their culture. The modern world is still suffering from the native incapacity of the Jews to be political. The art of making and preserving a City, which we call by the Greek name, ' politics,' was never an indigenous growth among the Hebrews. The City of the Greeks and the other civilized nations of anti-quity was hateful to them. Their ideas were essentially anti-political. The politics of Judæa, when there were any, were borrowed from the Egyptians and Babylonians and, later, from the Greeks. These borrowings were regarded with violent disapproval by the champions of Hebrew orthodoxy, who objected to organized civiliza-tion on two grounds. Some, like Amos, hated it just because it *was* civilization and not nomadic barbarism. It was in the desert that God had made his covenant with the Chosen Race, and in the desert there was nothing else to think about but God. So, Back to the Desert ! was their war-cry. Others, the Ebionites, objected to civilization because it was hierarchical, because it made for social inequality. They gave pro-phetically indignant utterance to the envious hatred of the poor in cash and in spirit against the rich and talented and cultured. A pious and universal mediocrity was their ideal.

The spiritual descendants of these two classes of prophets are still with us. What Amos said so many centuries ago, Gandhi and the Tol-

stoyans are saying to-day. The Communists are
the modern Ebionites. And this resemblance
between the old and the new is not a chance resemblance. But for the Bible, Tolstoy would never
have come to think as he did ; and Lenin was the
disciple of that old-fashioned Hebrew prophet in
scientific fancy dress, Karl Marx. The Hellenic
City has found in these Jew-inspired leaders and
their followers some of its bitterest enemies.

The Jews were also responsible, at any rate in
part, for an even more pernicious anti-political
doctrine—the doctrine of the all-importance in
human life of economic success. That prosperity was, or ought to be, the reward of virtue
was a fundamental article of the Jewish creed.
Why are the Bad sometimes Rich ? That, for
the Jews, was the principal Riddle of the Universe. There was only one God, and he existed
primarily to see that the virtuous were successful.
The Bible-reading Protestants, especially Calvin,
introduced this idea into Europe. The Puritans
were the first typically modern Business Men—
the first rich Christians who were not slightly
ashamed and frightened of being rich ; the first
shopkeepers to feel themselves the equals of
gentlemen, artists, scholars, priests (and not
merely their equals, but even their superiors) ;
the first mechanics who ever esteemed their
money-getting as a pursuit to be ranked with
contemplation and the liberal arts. It is in the
essentially Protestant America — home of the

ignoble Benjamin Franklin—that this Jewish
doctrine of the primacy of economic values has
found the widest acceptance and been most
whole-heartedly acted upon. From America
it has begun to infect the rest of the world.
Thanks to the Protestant Reformers, the whole
of humanity is being Judaized. We are all
paying for ' l'extrême simplicité de l'esprit
sémitique.'

Having made what is obviously an utterly
damning statement about the Chosen Race and
its religion, Renan calmly proceeds to explain
that the mission, the historical ' point,' of the
Jews was to tend the small flame of monotheism
and to transmit it, in due course and by the
agency of the first Christians, to the Western
world. Their mission, in a word, was to infect
the rest of humanity with a belief which, according to Renan himself, prevented them from
having any art, any philosophy, any political life,
any breadth or diversity of vision, any progress.
We may be pardoned for wishing that the Jews
had remained, not forty, but four thousand
years in their repulsive wilderness.

If the effects of pure monotheism are really
those which Renan attributes to it, then, it is
obvious, the passage from the worship of many
Gods to the worship of one cannot possibly be
called a progress, at any rate in the sphere of
practical living. An enthusiastic monotheist
will retort that progress in the art of life is not

' true ' progress, and that the only progress worth considering is that towards the Truth. ' Monotheism,' he would argue, ' may be incompatible with art, philosophy, political life, and all the rest. I am ready to grant your whole case. Nevertheless, I would rather believe in one God and be a barren Semite—a spiritual desert roaming through deserts of sand—than be a fertile Greek and believe in many Gods. For monotheism is *true* and polytheism is *false*.' But such a statement, as we have seen, is quite meaningless. Monotheism and polytheism are the rationalizations of distinct psychological states, both undeniably existent as facts of experience, and between which it is quite impossible for us, with the merely human faculties at our disposal, to choose. Any particular system of polytheism may fairly safely be regarded as untrue, or at any rate highly improbable. It is highly improbable, for example, that Thor or Dionysus ever existed in the same way as Mount Olympus or the Atlantic Ocean existed and continue to exist. Their being is of the same kind as the being of Jehovah and the something not ourselves that made for nineteenth-century righteousness, as the being of the unicorn and the Economic Man and the absolutely equilateral triangle. (Whether the two forms of existence are radically and essentially different is another question. Both are existences in a mind : but one type of existence seems to have a closer connection with a hypothetical outside world of things in themselves than the other. Are we justified in drawing a definite distinction, except for the purely practical purposes of our daily living, between the two classes of existence ? It is difficult to say.) That Thor or Dionysus ever 'really' existed is, I repeat, exceedingly improbable—though there is, of course, no conceivable method of proving that they did not or do not now exist, just as there is no conceivable method of disproving the existence of those disembodied spirits who were once supposed to direct the movements of the planets. At any moment Aphrodite may suddenly rise from the waves at Bournemouth or St. Leonards. *May* rise ; but, alas, how much more probably may not ! There is every reason to fear that life in these delicious resorts will continue to moulder away undisturbed towards some final and unattainable state of Absolute Putrefaction. But though the 'real' existence of the deities of any pantheon may be doubted, the existence of the internal and external diversity of which they are symbolical is undeniable. No less undeniable is the existence of some kind of inward and outward unity. But that this unity should really be the God of pure monotheism is as improbable as that the diversity should really be Apollo and Quexalcoatl, Siva and Thor.

For a certain class of highly civilized men and women, any passage from the concrete to the abstract, from the sensed and the felt to the merely thought about, is a progress. The man whose activities are predominantly intellectual, who lives mainly with and for disembodied ideas, is regarded by these people (they are, of course, paying a graceful compliment to themselves) as a being of a higher type than the man who lives to any considerable extent with the instinctive, intuitive, and passional side of his nature in a world of immediate experiences and concrete things. (In the sphere of practical living, as we have seen, the distinction, perhaps invalid theoretically, between the class of psychological facts which we call ' the concrete ' and that other class which we call ' the abstract ' is of the highest significance, and must therefore be clearly drawn.) To intellectuals of the kind I have described, polytheism seems a debased form of religion ; its many Gods too faithfully symbolize the diversities of the external world and of the instinctive and passional side of human nature. A single, infinite, disembodied divinity is much more to their taste. For a long time, however, this God remains too grossly personal and, despite his infiniteness, anthropomorphic to be wholeheartedly accepted by minds that are only perfectly at ease with algebraical symbols. The process of slow mangling and gradual murder, which these people beautifully call 'the spiritualization of man's conception of the divine,' must be carried to its extreme limit. Long since castrated, the deity must now be bled and disembowelled.

Only when the last drop of living blood has been squeezed from the eternal arteries does God become fit to be worshipped by a high-class intellectual modernist. For by this time God has degenerated into an algebraical formula, a pure abstraction. He is no longer alive, no longer has the least connection with life ; he has become simply a word *et præterea nihil*. When he said that the Word was in the beginning, St. John made a slight mistake. ' At the end ' was what he should have written. By the time he has been reduced to a mere verbal abstraction, God is at his last gasp. The modernists have all but spiritualized him out of existence. From polytheism to monotheism, from monotheism to the worship of an abstraction, from the worship of an abstraction to the worship of nothing at all —such are the several stages in the progressive ' spiritualization of man's conception of the divine.' And perhaps the process may turn out in the end to have been genuinely progressive— progressive in a circle or perhaps a spiral. For, who knows ? the nihilistic atheism into which advancing spirituality is so rapidly leading us may prove to be the introduction, by the way of almost desperate reaction, to a new and more perfect polytheism, itself the symbolical expression of a new and affirmative attitude towards those divinely mysterious forces of Life against which we now so ungratefully blaspheme. But before going further with these speculations

about the future and the possible, I must turn
aside to say something, in the most general terms,
about the actual history of that monotheism
which the Western peoples took over from the
Jews.

## § 6. *Trees and Fruits*

If what Renan says about the sterilizing effects
of pure monotheism be true (as I think it is),
how are we to explain the fact that the races of
Europe have not sunk, since their conversion,
to the level of those deplorable Semites, among
whom their historian could find no art, no science,
no philosophy, no politics, none of those activities,
in a word, which justify men in taking a certain
pride in their humanity ? The tree shall be
known by its fruits. Christian Europe has borne
good fruits in plenty. Are these the fruits of its
monotheism ? No. The peoples whom the
Jews infected with their monotheism were by
long tradition profoundly polytheistic. They
lived, moreover, in a world that was not a desert,
a world not barren, hard and dry, but softly alive
with the most various richness. They have
never, until quite recent times, shown any signs
of becoming pure monotheists, like their Semitic
teachers. Christian orthodoxy itself made a
compromise with polytheism. Its one God was
mysteriously several Gods. It encouraged the
worship of a subsidiary female deity. Innumerable saints received their tribute of local adora-

tion, usurped the place once occupied by the
lares and penates in the home, and provided with
their relics an inexhaustible supply of fetishes.
(Not quite inexhaustible, however. The demand
sometimes outran the supply ; Chaucer's Par-
doner was compelled to travel with a glass case
full of ' pigges bones.') In quantity the Catholic
could rival with any heathen pantheon known to
history. But not in quality. That was bad.
For the saints were drearily lacking in variety ;
they were all monotonously ' good.' For all
their swarming numbers, they represented but
one aspect of human life—the ' spiritual.' The
Greek and all the other professedly polytheistic
systems were much completer, much more
realistic. Their pantheons contained representatives of every vital activity—representatives of
the body and the instincts as well as of the spirit,
of the passionate energies as well as of the reason,
of the self-regarding as well as of the altruistic
tendencies in human nature. True, the Christians did recognize the existence of these other,
unspiritual aspects of existence ; but they handed
them over for symbolical embodiment to the
Devil and his angels. Most of the virtues of the
pagans—beauty, strength, cunning, and all such
wisdom as is not the inspired imbecility of the
poor in spirit—were branded as vices and attributed to the Prince of this World. The result
of this astonishing policy was the implanting in
the modern soul of all that strange and repulsive

24

gamut of peculiarly Christian diseases, from diabolism to conviction of sin, from the Folly of the Cross to Don-Juanism. What had once been a frank worship of the Gods of Life degenerated, during the Christian era, into a furtive and self-consciously guilty practice of devil-worship. Christianity could not destroy the old Adam ; it merely perverted him and made him disgusting.

That men with souls so *naturaliter non Christianæ* as the Greeks, the Romans, and, later, the other peoples of Europe, should ever have accepted Jewish monotheism, even in the impure form in which it was offered them by Christianity, may seem surprising. But, as it happened, circumstances in the first centuries of our era were extremely propitious to the spread of Semitic dogmas in the West. If Gods are made in the image of men, cosmogonies reflect the forms of terrestrial states. In an empire ruled absolutely by one man the notion of an universe under the control of a single God seemed obvious and reasonable. When the world was divided up into small states ruled by noble oligarchies, the idea was not reasonable nor obvious. The Christian God was a magnified and somewhat flattering portrait of Tiberius and Caligula.

Under the Roman Empire, the Western world was unified. The process entailed the destruction, or at least the reduction to insignificant impotence, of all the old nobilities. There was a general levelling down of castes. Under its absolute monarch the Empire was in some sort a democracy. Class distinctions came to depend more and more exclusively on wealth. The Best Men were the richest. Hereditary aristocracies, heaven knows, are bad enough ; but plutocracies are worse. Even degenerate aristocracies preserve a certain decency ; but at no time does a plutocracy develop any decency worth preserving : its *Weltanschauung* is uniformly detestable. Plutocrats are believers either in a sordid Franklinesque morality (the Puritans, it is significant, were the first modern capitalists) ; or in a no less sordid self-indulgence ; or in both at once. The Gospel of Work and the Gospel of the Good Time are equally popular in the modern world. A genuine aristocracy would find them equally stupid and disgusting.

Among the old aristocracies, destroyed by the Roman Empire, polytheism was the traditional religion. The Gods were the images of the ruling nobles projected through the magnifying, the beautifully distorting medium of the imagination on to the vault of heaven.

The cardinal virtues, in these ancient societies, were the virtues of a class of masters. The deadly sins (but they were neither deadly nor sins, in the Christian sense, but only contemptible defects of mind and body) were the characteristic failings of slaves. With the rise of the Empire, the ruling castes slowly withered. Between the monarch and the swarming slaves only the semblance of a nobility and the sordid reality of a class of money-makers now intervened. Freed from the aristocratic tradition, which had imposed on them its alien ethic and beliefs, the slaves now found themselves in a position to express their religious preferences. They chose the religion which assured them that they alone were virtuous in this life, and would alone be happy in the next ; the religion that exalted pity as the first of duties and condemned power as the worst of crimes ; the religion that proclaimed the equality of all men, that preached universal love and at the same time (for the love was tempered by envy and hatred) promised the weak a posthumous vengeance on their masters. In a word, they chose Christianity. Its monotheism, its universalism, fitted the imperial circumstances. In due course it became the religion of the State.[1] Shortly, however, after this event, the circumstances which had made possible the spread of the new religion entirely changed. The religion of slaves was required to adapt itself to an aristocratic society.

The revival of aristocracy was due to the Barbarians, who broke up the Empire and created a class of land-holding magnates to rule over the

[1] All this is perhaps a little too ‘ profound ’ in the German manner. But for Constantine’s whim, would Christianity ever have become the State religion ? Similarly, would England have taken to Protestantism if Henry had been less anxious to get rid of his wife ? Such questions are obviously unanswerable. But when generalizations become too ‘ profound,’ they are always worth asking.

fragments. Even before the destruction of the imperial machine we can detect signs that presage the coming feudal system. By the end of the fourth century the great landowners were full-blown barons, above the imperial law. The State could do nothing against them ; it was too weak, because too poor, to be able to oppress any but the feeble. That the once incredibly wealthy Empire should have sunk into such poverty may seem at a first sight inexplicably strange. But the Romans had squandered unproductively all the vast sums they had won by their Eastern conquests. Of capitalism in the modern form they were quite ignorant. Rome had no industries, and its financiers were merely usurers. The economic collapse of Rome began as early as the second century. Money became scarcer and scarcer ; barter and payment in kind—all the most rudimentary forms of economic activity— were gradually reintroduced. One of the results of this process was that the plutocracy of the Empire's palmy days began to transform itself into an aristocracy, for aristocracy flourishes where economic conditions are simple. When they become more complicated, a plutocracy takes its place. But not at once. There is a period when plutocrat and aristocrat exist and rule side by side—when the aristocrat is enriched by commerce and industry and the new plutocrat tries to live in accord with the old aristocratic tradition. These transitional periods have been the most splendid in human history. Athens and Florence at the height of their glory were each in this transitional state. So was England during the sixteenth and, diminishingly, the seventeenth and eighteenth centuries. So was France at the same epoch. So was Germany during the eighteenth century. But this happy state has never lasted for very long. Either some catastrophe puts a sudden end to it (as was the case with Athens and Florence) ; or else it develops gradually and naturally into something different, something worse. Plutocracy gains on aristocracy and at last displaces it altogether ; a new type of society comes into existence, and with it a new civilization. The world of Pericles and Lorenzo the Magnificent becomes the world of Hoover and Ford.

I can observe how a piece of phosphorus behaves when it is dry, and afterwards I can drop it in a pail of water and observe how it behaves when it is wet. But though I can observe (very incompletely and superficially, indeed) what happened as a result of Wellington's victory at Waterloo, I cannot alter the historical circumstances experimentally and observe what would have happened if Napoleon had won the battle. There can be no crucial experiments in history, nor, for that matter, any completely accurate observation. History is not a science.

What would have happened during the Dark Ages and the succeeding centuries, if the religion of Europe had not been monotheistic ? We cannot discover, we find it hard even to imagine. Conceivably, of course, the history of those times would have been the same as that which is actually recorded in the text-books. It seems, however, unlikely ; and I think we are justified in believing that monotheism played an important and, on the whole, beneficent part during those times, first of obscure tumult and then of piecemeal order. The monotheistic idea, with which were inextricably twined the catholic and imperial ideas, acted as a brake on those disruptive and centrifugal forces which might, but for it, have kept all Europe in a state of fragmentary chaos. Christianity, the preacher of monotheism, was valuable. But no less valuable, it should be remembered, was Christianity, the preserver of the old polytheistic culture. From the Jews Catholicism borrowed one God. From the Greeks and Romans it took all the rich diversity of art and thought which the Jews had sacrificed to their one God. What it had taken it passed on. For both its gifts, divided and barbarous Europe owed it an enormous debt of gratitude.

The circumstances of the Dark and Middle Ages rendered Christian monotheism, on the whole, a blessing and prevented it from doing harm. In a world broken up into isolated and politically independent fragments men could not take the idea of cosmic unity with dangerous seriousness. Moreover, the morality current in an aristocratic and warlike society was necessarily incompatible with Christian morality and served as a wholesome antidote to it. Nor must it be forgotten that religion was, for the great majority, an affair predominantly of formalities and fetish-worship. If you went through the formalities and worshipped the fetishes, it did not much matter what you did in the intervals. Men made little attempt to be consistently ' spiritual.' The few who took Christian teaching seriously could go into the monasteries and be spiritual in private. As for the rest, one has only to read the mediæval story-tellers to see what their way of life was like. In the golden ages of faith, most Christians lived, most of the time, in a manner almost as charmingly pagan as that of the ancient Cretans or Etruscans. The Age of Faith was golden (by comparison with that of militant Protestantism and the Counter-Reformation) because the faithful never dreamed of being consistently Christian.

The Renaissance was a revival of the polytheistic spirit. The parallel Reformation was a revival of pure Semitism. The Reformers read their Old Testaments and, trying to imitate the Jews, became those detestable Puritans to whom we owe, not merely Grundyism and Podsnappery, but also (as Weber and Tawney have shown) all that was and still is vilest, cruellest, most anti-human in the modern capitalist system. To their

31

one Jewish God good Calvinists and Independents sacrificed almost everything that could make a man prouder of being a man than of being a termite or a perfectly efficient automaton.

The Reformers took monotheism very seriously. A little later the triumphs of physical science led to its being taken no less seriously on other than religious grounds. Voltaire, for example, was an ardent monotheist, not because he wanted to be like the Jews, but because Sir Isaac Newton had successfully formulated, in terms of mathematical equations, a number of apparently changeless Laws of Nature. ‘God said, Let Newton be, and there was . . . God.’ The physicists, it seemed, had seen through the illusion of diversity ; the world was one and, with it, the world’s Creator. In due course Voltaire’s God became an abstraction, and as an abstraction, a word, he still presides, very remotely, over the destinies of most serious-minded people at the present time.

## § 7. *The Present*

The contemporary circumstances are even more propitious to the spread of monotheism than were those of the Roman Empire. What the imperial administration did for the Mediterranean basin and Western Europe, commerce and good communications, cheap printing and elementary education for all, the cinema and the radio, have done for the world at large. In spite of national antagonisms, we are aware of a certain planetary unity. It is an unity, at present, merely of economic interests ; and perhaps it will never be more than that. To me, at any rate, it seems in the highest degree unlikely that mankind will ever feel itself intimately and livingly one. The differences of race and place are too enormous. The blood of Europeans pulses to a rhythm of life that is not the same as the rhythm of Indian or Chinese or Negro blood. And the various climates and continents impose a variety of existence. A northerner can never feel as a man of the tropics feels ; America imposes a mode of being that is radically unlike the modes of being possible in the Old World. There is such a thing as absolute alienness. An absolute alienness which no amount of Esperanto and international government, of movies and thousand-miles-an-hour aeroplanes and standardized education, will ever, it seems to me, completely abolish.

Meanwhile, however, economic unity exists and men are aware of their common interests, just as under the Romans they were aware of their common servitude to a single master. The social circumstances are propitious to monotheism. But propitious circumstances are not creative, only fertilizing ; there must be a psychological seed for the circumstances to be propitious to. In our contemporary world, what is the seed of monotheism ?

For a section of the modern slave population Christianity is still the introduction to monotheism. But only for a section. Most slaves at the present time are not Christian at all. They are either too well off to feel the need of a consolatory faith—(witness the transformation of Christianity in America from a religion predominantly concerned with other-worldly virtues and posthumous revenges into a system for the justification of wealth and the preaching of industrious respectability ; from a system that condemned the Pharisee—that shining example of Good Citizenship—into one that exalts the Pharisee above every other human type)—either, I repeat, they are too prosperous to be Christians, or else, if they are badly off and discontented, they turn to one of the political surrogates of Christianity and find in communism and dreams of terrestrial Utopias a comforting prospect of happiness for themselves and condign punishment for their enemies. (From a political point of view, one of the great merits of Christianity is that it persuades the discontented to seek the cause of their woes, not in the surrounding social system, not in the crimes of their rulers, but in their own sinful natures and the divine order of the universe. For the English working classes the early years of the industrial epoch were years of unspeakable misery and degradation. Yet there was no revolution in England. For that we have largely to thank the

Methodists. These single-minded revivalists of Christianity did more to preserve the stability of English institutions than all the Tory politicians. The greatest conservatives of the age were not the Wellesleys, but the Wesleys.)

Contemporary monotheism—that vague and secular doctrine of the divine unity, which is now taken for granted as a sort of axiomatic truism—has its main psychological source in what, for lack of a better name, may be called our intellectualism. Not that we are all intellectuals nowadays. Far from it. But still less are we all predominantly instinctive, passional, intuitive beings. Instinct, passion, intuition are hindrances rather than helps to efficient citizenship of the contemporary world. We are members of a very highly organized society, in which it pays best to be either a man who understands and unremittingly wills, or else a kind of obedient automaton. Inevitably ; for the more complicated the social machine, the more inhumanly and mechanically simple becomes the task of the subordinate individual, the more inhumanly difficult that of the commanding organizer. Those who wish to lead a quiet life in our modern world must be like Babbitt—unquestioningly a cog. Those who are ambitious to lead a (by current standards) successful life must be like Ford, determined and very consciously intelligent. Those who would lead a thoroughly disastrous life have only to model themselves on the

35

pattern, shall we say, of Burns or William Blake. In a society like ours the successful are those who live intensely with the intellectual and voluntary side of their being, and as little as possible with the rest of themselves. The quietly Good Citizens are those who live as little as possible on any plane of existence. While those who live fully and harmoniously with their whole being are doomed to almost certain social disaster.

Triumphant science enhances the already enormous prestige of will-directed intelligence. The most ignorant member of the modern slave population would probably agree with Aristotle that the pursuit of knowledge is the highest duty and that the only permissible excesses are excesses of the intellect.

The intellectual, scientific knowledge of things which we now esteem so highly is a knowledge of the unity which underlies, at any rate in our minds, the manifold diversity of the world. Direct, living knowledge of diversity is not, by social and scientific standards, useful knowledge. There is also a direct intuitive knowledge of unity ; but it comes to us but rarely. At most times, and by most people, unity is apprehended after the fact by the abstracting intellect. For practical and scientific purposes the direct, or mystical, knowledge of unity is as useless as the direct knowledge of diversity.

The value of direct knowledge, as I shall try to show later on, consists in the fact that it is a

stimulator, a nourisher of life. Between the two
kinds of knowledge—the direct physical knowledge, whether of diversity or of unity, and the
intellectual knowledge, abstracted and general-
ized out of this physical knowledge—is a difference analogous to that between food and an
instrument. Knives and hammers are indispensable ; but so, to an even higher degree, is
bread. Our present tendency is to overvalue
the instrument and to undervalue the food which
alone can give us the vital power and health to
use the instrument properly. Contemporary
monotheism is an expression of our excessive
love for that abstract knowledge of the general
and the uniform which enables us to explain
and predict and organize and do many other
useful things, but gives us, alas ! no sustenance
by which we may live.

### § 8. *Pragmatic Sanctions*

My theme so far has been monotheism as truth
or falsehood, and monotheism as a historical fact.
The time has now come to consider the rights and
wrongs of monotheism, its usefulness or the
reverse, its conformity or nonconformity to the
facts of human nature.

Of monotheism's conformity to the psychological facts—of its inward as opposed to its outward truth—I have already said something. Let
me recapitulate in a rather different key. We

can affirm that the universe, with its divinity, is one, founding our belief on the fact that we have had a direct experience of its unity. But in this case we must ignore all the much more numerous occasions when we have had a direct experience of its diversity. True, the mystics are never tired of affirming that their direct perceptions of unity are intenser, of finer quality and intrinsically more convincing, more self-evident, than their direct perceptions of diversity. But they can only speak for themselves. Other people's direct intuitions of diverse ' appearances ' may be just as intensely self-evident as *their* intuition of unique ' reality.' Not only may be, but evidently are—that is, if we can judge by the artistic statements of their experiences made by talented unity-perceivers and talented diversity-perceivers respectively. (And we have no other means of judging.) The final mystery is unknowable. Men's confused perceptions of it are diverse and contradictory. The truth—the inward truth, I mean, since that is the only truth we can know—is that God is different for different men, and for the same man on different occasions. The testimony of the mystics cannot be made to prove more than this. Nor can that of the discursive reasoners. For if we arrive at our notion of divine unity by a process of discursive reasoning after the event, we find ourselves forced to affirm that one psychological fact (in this case of an intellectual kind) is ' truer ' than another (of a sensuous kind). An assumption for which, as we have already seen, there is no justification, but which has nevertheless been made by many philosophers, from Plato onwards and downwards. It is an attractive assumption, and one which flatters human weakness. For immediately apprehended reality is inextricably bewildering to the conscious and purposive thinker. It is only in a home-made universe of abstractions that men can feel thoroughly at home. How gratifying to think that this cosy little world of ideas is ' truer ' than the vast and shifting incoherency of surrounding appearances ! And to know that one's own pet universe is also God's pet universe, that one's own elegant world of words is the world of the Word with a large W : what a source of legitimate pride, and what a comfort ! One is not surprised at Plato's popularity.

But one psychological fact is as good as another ; there is no conceivable method of demonstrating that God is either one or many. So far as human beings are concerned, he is both ; monotheism and polytheism are equally true. But are they equally useful ? Do they tend equally to the quickening and enhancement of human life ? (I am assuming—it is an act of faith—that more and intenser life is preferable to less and feebler life.)

Let us put the questions in more general, more fundamentally psychological terms. Monotheism and polytheism are more or less systematic rationalizations of a sentiment of our own and the world's unity and a sentiment of our own and the world's diversity, respectively. Which is the more valuable for life—the unity-feeling with its various religious or philosophical rationalizations, or the diversity-feeling with *its* attendant doctrines?

## § 9. *The Two Kinds of Knowledge*

Men are also citizens; there are no Crusoes. In a highly organized society, however, the citizens are apt to forget that they are also men. They come to value themselves and their fellows for what they can do in a socially useful way—as personified functions rather than as human beings. They admire those who are well provided with that kind of knowledge which I have called instrumental. For those who have grown strong on the knowledge that is life's nourishment, they have no particular respect; on the contrary, they often despise and, at the same time, mistrust and fear them.

Files and screwdrivers are not the most satisfactory articles of diet. Analogously, there is no psychical nourishment to be drawn from the abstract, instrumental knowledge so much appreciated in a society like our own. Souls are nourished only by a direct participative knowledge of things, by an immediate physical contact, by a relationship involving will, desire, feeling. (And, incidentally, if those who pursue instrumental knowledge do sometimes succeed in deriving a kind of nourishment from their files and screwdrivers, that is due to the fact that they are filled with a passion for these tools, that they pursue their abstractions with appetite and a sort of sensuality.)

Direct participative knowledge is mostly a knowledge of diversity. Neglecting for the moment the mystic's direct participative knowledge of unity, we can say that the human spirit is mainly nourished by the multiplicity of the world. We incorporate this multiplicity into our substance ; it becomes part of ourselves. *Gnosce teipsum :* the commandment can only be obeyed on condition that we know, participatively know, the multiple world. For it is essentially the same with the mind as with the body. These fields of potatoes and cabbages, these browsing sheep and oxen, are potentially a part of me ; and unless they actually become part of me, I die. My future activity is green, is woolly, manures and is manured, says baa, says moo, says nothing at all. The apparent boundaries of any real being are not its real boundaries. We all think we know what a lion is. A lion is a desert-coloured animal with a mane and claws and an expression like Garibaldi's. But it is also, in Africa, all the neighbouring antelopes and zebras, and therefore, indirectly, all the neighbouring grass. It is also, behind the menagerie bars, all the superannuated

41

horses that come into the local market. In the same way, a human spirit is all that it can experience. Its boundaries are even more indefinitely wide than those of the corporeal man. The whole experienceable world is potentially a part of it, just as the whole edible or otherwise physically assimilable world is a part, potentially, of the body. But the body remains, for all practical purposes, the same, whatever, within limits, the food that nourishes it. The spirit, on the other hand, can be profoundly modified by that which it assimilates. Certain experiences will alter the relative importance of the elements composing the soul, will suddenly waken what had been asleep and violently actualize what had been only latent hitherto and potential. Changes which, if they happened to the body, would be miraculous, are everyday occurrences in the world of the spirit. No man can know himself completely, for the good reason that no man can have had all possible experiences and therefore can never have realized all the potentialities of his being. The man who spends his time trying, introspectively, to ' know himself ' discovers less than any one else. Necessarily. For there is less for him to discover. Self-limited, his sole experience a kind of spiritual onanism, he only partially exists. If there were no antelopes and zebras there would be no lion. When the supply of game runs low, the king of beasts grows thin and mangy ; it ceases altogether, and he dies.

So with the soul. Its principal food is the direct,
the physical experience of diversity.

Certain philosophers deliberately reduce the
food supply. ' " Do you think it like a philosopher to take very seriously what are called
pleasures, such as eating and drinking ? " " Certainly not, Socrates," said Simmias.' (How one's
feet itch to kick the bottoms of these imbeciles
who always agree with the old sophist, whatever
nonsense he talks ! They deserved the hem-
lock even more richly than their master.) ' " Or
sex ? " ' Socrates goes on. ' " No." " Or the
whole business of looking after the body ? Will
the philosopher rate that highly ? " ' Of course
he won't—the fool ! The philosopher's soul
' withdraws itself as far as it can from all associa-
tion and contact with the body and reaches
out after truth by itself.' With what results ?
Deprived of its nourishment, the soul grows thin
and mangy, like the starved lion. Disgusted and
pitying in the midst of our admiration, ' Poor
brutes ! ' we cry at the sight of such extraordinary
and lamentable souls as those of Kant, of Newton,
of Descartes. ' Why aren't they given enough
to eat ? '

The ascetics go even further than the philosophers. They starve their souls to death—or,
in more orthodox language, detach themselves
completely from all earthly things. Ceasing to
perceive, to think, to feel, to desire, to act, the
more mystical among them fall into that state

of ecstatic coma when the blank and empty spirit is said to be united with the Infinite—in other words, when it has ceased to be alive. The more practical ascetics—reformers or reactionary soldiers of the church militant—galvanize their death into a gruesome activity with the stimulus of some monomaniacal principle, some insanely fixed idea.

Philosophers and ascetics are not, of course, the only people who commit self-murder. The money-grubber, the hard-headed business man, the routine-worker, pass their existence no less suicidally. The professional Don Juan destroys his spirit as fatally as does the professional ascetic, whose looking-glass image he is. To live, the soul must be in intimate contact with the world, must assimilate it through all the channels of sense and desire, thought and feeling, which nature has provided for the purpose. Anything which obstructs these channels injures the soul— any deadening routine, any dull habitual un- awareness, any exclusive monomania, whether of vice or of that other vice which is excessive virtue. Close up enough of these channels, cut off enough of its nourishment, and the starved soul dies.

Dead souls, like dead bodies, either shrivel up into dry and dusty mummies, or else, decaying, they stink. What an unbearable stench arises, for example, from the Thebaid! One must hold one's nose when one reads Palladius's history. Calvin's Geneva is another open sewer. So is the Paris of De Nerciat's Felicia. So are Podsnap's London and Babbitt's Zenith. The odour of Marie Alacoque's sanctity is enough to give one typhoid. Even in Pascal's neighbourhood there is a bit of a smell. Other dead souls do not damply rot, but wither almost aromatically into desiccation. About many scholars, for example, there hangs no worse an odour than that of dust and old bindings. There are certain saints who have dried up into a condition of powdery fragrance, like lavender between the sheets in a linen-cupboard. Positively a pleasant smell. But I for one prefer the moist, still earthy perfume of the flowers on the growing plant that has its roots deep burrowing and darkly living in the soil.

Life, then, individual life, is mainly nourished by the direct participative knowledge of the world's diversity. Out of that diversity, and out of the inner diversity of the human spirit, the poetic imagination of man extracts the deities of polytheism. And the rites of their worship are man's participative knowledge and man's emotional reactions to the world, systematized in a set of words and gestures. The ritual of Catholicism is a maimed version of polytheistic ritual— maimed, because it systematizes only a part of man's emotional reactions to the world, because it ignores, or brands as evil, certain kinds of participative knowledge of certain whole classes of things. Every dionysiac reaction to the world, every corybantic participation of individual energies with the energies of living nature, has been proscribed. The Catholic ritual canalizes only a part of the human responses to the universe, just as the Christian God symbolically represents only a part of the psychological and cosmic reality.

The intuitive or intellectual realization of cosmic unity, the religious and philosophical systems which impose this cosmic unity as a necessary dogma, possess, for man, a predominantly social and scientific value. Without some unifying hypothesis, without generalizations and abstractions, organized knowledge is impossible. Social relations would be equally impossible, if men did not believe in some sort of community of tribal, national, and finally human interests, or were without a conception of their own psychological unity and that of their fellows. The Gods symbolize, and at the same time confirm, the community of their worshippers' interests. The conception of the individual soul, single, persistent, and responsible, is at once an expression and a guarantee of man's individual and social morality.

## § 10. *Conclusions*

Monotheism and polytheism are doctrines equally necessary and equally true. Man can and does conceive of himself and of the world

46

as being, now essentially many, and now essentially one. Therefore—since God, for our human purposes, is simply Life in so far as man can conceive it as a whole—the Divine is both one and many. A purely monotheistic religion is thus seen to be inadequate and unrealistic. The present age is predominantly monotheistic—monotheistic either because it feebly believes in a decaying Christianity, or else secularly and irreligiously monotheistic, with the unitarianism of science, of democracy, of international capitalism. In the interests of the Man as opposed to the Citizen (and incidentally in the interests of the Citizen too—for you cannot ruin the individual without, in the long run, ruining society) it has become necessary to protest against this now pernicious doctrine. Tempering what would have been, in the dark ages of chaotic barbarism, a dangerous cult of diversity, the worship of one God was doubtless, in its time, an admirable thing. Times have changed ; monotheism has lost the value which circumstances once gave it. It lacks political utility, and to the individual it is a poison. Even in its worst days polytheism never degenerated, as monotheism has done, into bloodless religious spirituality on the one hand, and an irreligious worship, on the other, of no less bloodless intellectual abstractions and mechanical efficiency. The sterile creed of the ascetic has to a great extent given place, in our modern world, to the sterile creeds of the

47

abstraction-worshipping man of science and the machine-worshipping man of applied science (who is the modern 'average man'). Indeed, Christian spirituality prepared the way for our intellectualism and machine-worship by rendering disreputable all that in human nature is not mind, not spirit, not conscious will. The established religion decayed ; but the philosophical and ethical habits which it had generated mouldering·ly persisted and persist. The high-minded man who would, in the past, have been an earnest Christian, is now—what ? Not an earnest (or preferably light-hearted) pagan, but an earnest intellectual, living ascetically for knowledge. And the low-minded man ? He is no ascetic, of course, and his goal is not knowledge, but money, comfort, and a 'good time.' The intellectual despises him for living grossly, on the plane of the body. The contempt is justified because he lives so inadequately and poorly on that plane. (If he lived well there, he would be a much better man than the intellectual.) Lacking all religious significance, his physical and instinctive life is pointless and rather dirty. It is also lamentably incomplete. By deconsecrating his body and the diverse world with which it participatively communicates through the instincts, feelings, and desires, by robbing them of their divine meaning, Christianity has left him without defence against our mechanized civilization. Rationalized division of labour takes all the sense out of his work. (For, as I have already pointed out, the more elaborately complicated the social organization, the more inhumanly and abjectly simple becomes the task of the individual.) Machines relieve him, not merely of drudgery, but of the possibility of performing any creative or spontaneous act whatsoever. And this is now true of his leisure as well as of his labour ; he has almost ceased even to try to divert himself, but sits and suffers a standardized entertainment to trickle over his passive consciousness. Amusements have been mechanized ; it is the latest and perhaps the most fatal triumph of our industrial-scientific civilization. By men with a religious sense of Life's divineness the inroads of this civilization would have been bitterly resented and stubbornly resisted. Not by Christians, however. Christianity had taught that the worship of any aspect of Life but the spiritual was a sin. Good pagans might have found a satisfactory method of dealing with the problems raised by the coming of the machine. Good Christians could hardly see that there were any problems to solve. Passively they accepted the evil thing. They accepted it because they did not see that it was evil. The machine had nothing to do with the body ; its function was to ' set the mind free for higher things.' It might be regarded, in fact, as a positively spiritual object.

The chief result of the preaching of Christian

49

spirituality and of its later substitutes, scientific intellectualism and business efficiency, is that men now instinctively and enthusiastically love the lowest when they see it. The apostles laboured, the martyrs died in torment, the philosophers thought sublime thoughts, by precept and example the scholars and the men of science proclaimed the beauties of the ' higher life,' the sociologists untiringly inculcated the duty of good citizenship, and all agreed that God is one and a spirit, and that man's first duty is to resemble God. To what end ? That men might become purer, they would have answered, better, more than men. But what has actually occurred ? Trying to live superhumanly, men have sunk, in all but the purely mental sphere, towards a kind of sub-humanity that it would be an undeserved compliment to call bestial. Turned against Life, they have worshipped Death in the form of spirituality, intellectualism, and at last mere efficiency. Deprived of the support of Life's divinities, they have succumbed to the shoddy temptations of the Devil of the Machine. By exhorting men to lead the ' higher life,' Christianity and its philosophical successors have condemned men to an existence incomparably lower than that ' low life ' against which they have always fulminated. To their cry of ' Excelsior ! ' humanity has responded (in the very nature of things it could not do otherwise) by rushing down a steep place into—what ? We who are only part way down the Gadarene water-chute are not as yet in a position to answer. The gulf lies dark before us, and stinking.

If men are ever to rise again from the depths into which they are now descending, it will only be with the aid of a new religion of life. And since life is diverse, the new religion will have to have many Gods. Many ; but since the individual man is an unity in his various multiplicity, also one. It will have to be Dionysian and Panic as well as Apollonian ; Orphic as well as rational ; not only Christian, but Martial and Venerean too ; Phallic as well as Minervan or Jehovahistic. It will have to be all, in a word, that human life actually is, not merely the symbolical expression of one of its aspects. Meanwhile, however, the Gadarene descent continues.

# SILENCE IS GOLDEN

I have just been, for the first time, to see and hear a picture talk. 'A little late in the day,' my up-to-date readers will remark, with a patronizing and contemptuous smile. 'This is 1929; there isn't much news in talkies now. But better late than never.'

Better late than never? Ah, no! There, my friends, you 're wrong. This is one of those cases where it is most decidedly better never than late, better never than early, better never than on the stroke of time. One of the numerous cases, I may add ; and the older I grow, the more numerous I find them. There was a time when I should have felt terribly ashamed of not being up-to-date. I lived in a chronic apprehension lest I might, so to speak, miss the last bus, and so find myself stranded and benighted in a desert of demodedness, while others, more nimble than myself, had already climbed on board, taken their tickets and set out towards those bright but, alas, ever receding goals of Modernity and Sophistication. Now, however, I have grown shameless, I have lost my fears. I can watch unmoved the departure of the last social-cultural bus—the innumerable last buses, which are starting at every instant in all the world's capitals. I make no effort to board them, and when the noise of each departure has died down, 'Thank Goodness ! ' is what I say to myself in the solitude. I find nowadays that I simply don't want to be up-to-date. I have lost all desire to see and do the things, the seeing and doing of which entitle a man to regard himself as superiorly knowing, sophisticated, unprovincial ; I have lost all desire to frequent the places and people that a man simply *must* frequent, if he is not to be regarded as a poor creature hopelessly out of the swim. ' Be up-to-date ! ' is the categorical imperative of those who scramble for the last bus. But it is an imperative whose cogency I refuse to admit. When it is a question of doing something which I regard as a duty, I am as ready as any one else to put up with discomfort. But being up-to-date and in the swim has ceased, so far as I am concerned, to be a duty. Why should I have my feelings outraged, why should I submit to being bored and disgusted, for the sake of somebody else's categorical imperative ? Why ? There is no reason. So I simply avoid most of the manifestations of that so-called ' life ' which my contemporaries seem to be so unaccountably anxious to ' see ' ; I keep out of range of the ' art ' they think it so vitally necessary to ' keep up with ' ; I flee from those ' good times,' in the ' having ' of which they are prepared to spend so lavishly of their energy and cash.

Such, then, are the reasons for my very tardy introduction to the talkies. The explanation of my firm resolve never, if I can help it, to be re-

introduced will be found in the following simple
narrative of what I saw and heard in that fetid
hall on the Boulevard des Italiens, where the
latest and most frightful creation-saving device
for the production of standardized amusement
had been installed.

We entered the hall half-way through the performance of a series of music-hall turns—not substantial ones, of course, but the two-dimensional
images of turns with artificial voices. There
were no travel films, nothing in the Natural
History line, none of those fascinating Events of
the Week—Lady Mayoresses launching battle-
ships, Japanese earthquakes, hundred-to-one out-
siders winning races, revolutionaries on the march
in Nicaragua—which are always the greatest and
often the sole attractions in the programmes of
our cinemas. Nothing but disembodied enter-
tainers, gesticulating flatly on the screen and
making gramophone-like noises as they did so.
Some sort of comedian was performing as we
entered. But he soon vanished to give place to
somebody's celebrated jazz-band—not merely
audible in all its loud vulgarity of brassy guffaw
and caterwauling sentiment, but also visible in a
series of apocalyptic close-ups of the individual
performers. A beneficent providence has dimmed
my powers of sight, so that at a distance of more
than four or five yards I am blissfully unaware
of the full horror of the average human countenance. At the cinema, however, there is no

escape. Magnified up to Brobdingnagian proportions, the human countenance smiles its six-foot smiles, opens and shuts its thirty-two-inch eyes, registers soulfulness or grief, libido or whimsicality, with every square centimetre of its several roods of pallid mooniness. Nothing short of total blindness can preserve one from the spectacle. The jazz-players were forced upon me ; I regarded them with a fascinated horror. It was the first time, I suddenly realized, that I had ever clearly *seen* a jazz-band. The spectacle was positively terrifying.

The performers belonged to two contrasted races. There were the dark and polished young Hebrews, whose souls were in those mournfully sagging, sea-sickishly undulating melodies of mother-love and nostalgia and yammering amorousness and clotted sensuality which have been the characteristically Jewish contributions to modern popular music. And there were the chubby young Nordics, with Aryan faces transformed by the strange plastic forces of the North American environment into the likeness of very large uncooked muffins or the unveiled posteriors of babes. (The more sympathetic Red Indian type of Nordic American face was completely absent from this particular assemblage of jazz-players.) Gigantically enlarged, these personages appeared one after another on the screen, each singing or playing his instrument, and at the same time registering the emotions appropri-

55

ate to the musical circumstances. The spectacle, I repeat, was really terrifying. For the first time I felt grateful for the defect of vision which had preserved me from an earlier acquaintance with such aspects of modern life. And at the same time I wished that I could become, for the occasion, a little hard of hearing. For if good music has charms to soothe the savage breast, bad music has no less powerful spells for filling the mildest breast with rage, the happiest with horror and disgust. Oh, those mammy-songs, those love-longings, those loud hilarities ! How was it possible that human emotions intrinsically decent could be so ignobly parodied ? I felt like a man who, having asked for wine, is offered a brimming bowl of hog-wash. And not even fresh hog-wash. Rancid hog-wash, decaying hog-wash. For there was a horrible tang of putrefaction in all that music. Those yearnings for Mammy of Mine and My Baby, for Dixie and the Land where Skies are Blue and Dreams come True, for Granny and Tennessee and You—they were all a necrophily. The Mammy after whom the black young Hebrews and the blond young muffin-faces so retchingly yearned was an ancient Gorgonzola cheese ; the Baby of their tremulously gargled desire was a leg of mutton after a month in warm storage ; Granny had been dead for weeks ; and as for Dixie and Tennessee and Dream Land— they were odoriferous with the least artificial of manures.

When, after what seemed hours, the jazz-band concluded its dreadful performance, I sighed in thankfulness. But the thankfulness was premature. For the film which followed was hardly less distressing. It was the story of the child of a Cantor in a synagogue, afflicted, to his father's justifiable fury, with an itch for jazz. This itch, assisted by the Cantor's boot, sends him out into the world, where, in due course, and thanks to My Baby, his dreams come tree-ue, and he is employed as a jazz-singer on the music-hall stage. Promoted from the provinces to Broadway, the jazz-singer takes the opportunity to revisit the home of his childhood. But the Cantor will have nothing to do with him, absolutely nothing, in spite of his success, in spite, too, of his moving eloquence. ' You yourself always taught me,' says the son pathetically, ' that the voice of music was the voice of God.' *Vox jazzi vox Dei*—the truth is new and beautiful. But stern old Poppa's heart refuses to be melted. Even Mammy of Mine is unable to patch up a reconciliation. The singer is reduced to going out once more into the night—and from the night back to his music-hall, where, amid a forest of waving legs, he resumes his interrupted devotions to that remarkable God whose voice is the music of Mr. Irving Berlin as interpreted by Mr. Paul Whiteman's orchestra.

The crisis of the drama arrives when, the Cantor being mortally sick and unable to fulfil his functions at the synagogue, Mammy of Mine and the Friends of his Childhood implore the young man to come and sing the Atonement Service in his father's place. Unhappily, this religious function is booked to take place at the same hour as that other act of worship vulgarly known as the First Night. There ensues a terrific struggle, worthy of the pen of a Racine or a Dryden, between love and honour. Love for Mammy of Mine draws the jazz-singer towards the synagogue; but love for My Baby draws the Cantor's son towards the theatre, where she, as principal Star, is serving the deity no less acceptably with her legs and smile than he with his voice. Honour also calls from either side ; for Honour demands that he should serve the God of his fathers at the synagogue, but it also demands that he should serve the jazz-voiced God of his adoption at the theatre. Some very eloquent captions appear at this point. With the air of a seventeenth-century hero, the jazz-singer protests that he must put his Career before even his love. The nature of the dilemma has changed, it will be seen, since Dryden's day. In the old dramas, it was love that had to be sacrificed to painful duty. In the modern instance the sacrifice is at the shrine of what William James called ' the Bitch Goddess, Success.' Love is to be abandoned for the stern pursuit of newspaper notoriety and dollars. The change is significant of the *Weltanschauung*, if not of the youngest

generation, at any rate of that which has passed
and is in process of passing. The youngest generation seems to be as little interested in careers
and money as in anything else, outside its own
psychology. But this is by the way.

In the end the singer makes the best of both
worlds—satisfies Mammy of Mine and even Poor
Poppa by singing at the synagogue, and, on the
following evening, scores a terrific success at the
postponed first night of My Baby's revue. The
film concludes with a scene in the theatre, with
Mammy of Mine in the stalls (Poor Poppa is by
this time safely underground), and the son, with
My Baby in the background, warbling down at
her the most nauseatingly luscious, the most
penetratingly vulgar mammy-song that it has
ever been my lot to hear. My flesh crept as the
loud-speaker poured out those sodden words,
that greasy, sagging melody. I felt ashamed of
myself for listening to such things, for even being
a member of the species to which such things are
addressed. But I derived a little comfort from
the reflection that a species which has allowed all
its instincts and emotions to degenerate and
putrefy in such a way must be pretty near either
its violent conclusion or else its radical transformation and reform.

To what length this process of decay has gone
was very strikingly demonstrated by the next item
on the programme, which was the first of that
series of music-hall turns of which the dreadful

jazz-band had been the last. For no sooner had the singer and My Baby and Mammy of Mine disappeared into the limbo of inter-cinemato-graphic darkness, than a very large and classically-profiled personage, dressed in the uniform of a clown, appeared on the screen, opened his mouth very wide indeed, and poured out, in a terrific Italian tenor voice, the famous soliloquy of Pagliacci from Leoncavallo's opera. Rum, Tum, Ti-Tum, Tum ; Rum-ti-ti, Tum, Ti-Tum, Tum—it is the bawling-ground of every Southern virtuoso, and a piece which, at ordinary times, I would go out of my way to avoid hearing. But in comparison with the jazz-band's Hebrew melodies and the singer's jovialities and mammy yearnings, Leoncavallo's throaty vulgarity seemed not only refined and sincere, but even beautiful, positively noble. Yes, noble ; for, after all, the composer, whatever his native second-rateness, had stood in some sort of organic relationship, through a tradition of taste and of feeling, with the men who built Santa Maria del Fiore and the Malatestan temple, who painted the frescoes at Arezzo and Padua, who composed the Mass of Pope Marcellus and wrote the Divine Comedy and the Orlando Furioso. Whereas the Hebrew melodists and the muffin-faced young Nordics, with their Swanee whistles and their saxophones, the mammy-songsters, the vocal yearners for Dixie and My Baby, are in no kind of relationship with any of the immemorial decencies of human life, but only with their own inward decay. It is a corruption as novel as the régime under which they and all the rest of us now live—as novel as protestantism and capitalism ; as novel as urbanization and democracy and the apotheosis of the Average Man ; as novel as Benjamin-Franklinism and the no less repulsive philosophy and ethic of the young Good Timer ; as novel as creation-saving machinery and the thought-saving, time-killing press ; as novel as Taylorized work and mechanized amusement. Ours is a spiritual climate in which the immemorial decencies find it hard to flourish. Another generation or so should see them definitely dead. Is there a resurrection ?

# SPINOZA'S WORM

"Let us imagine,' writes Spinoza, 'a little worm in the blood, which has vision enough to discern the particles of blood, lymph, etc., and reason enough to observe how one particle is repelled by another with which it comes in contact, or communicates a part of its motion to it. Such a worm would live in the blood as we do in this part of the universe, and would regard each particle of it, not as a part, but as a whole, nor could it know how all the parts are influenced by the universal nature of the blood and are obliged to accommodate themselves to each other as is required by that nature, so that they co-operate together according to a fixed law.' And so on. The gist of the matter—and it is the gist of all Spinoza's philosophy—is that we ought to live and move and have our being in the infinite, rather than the finite, that we should do our thinking in terms of the universal unity, not in terms of individual particulars. In a word, that we should cease to be worms in the blood and become—what? Butterflies, I suppose, winging freely through space.

Now, it would obviously be very agreeable to be a butterfly—more agreeable no doubt than to be a worm, even a worm in the rich warm blood. But, in practice and as a matter of observable fact, *can* worms transform themselves at will into

butterflies ? Is the miracle within their powers ?
I have met with no evidence to convince me that
it is. It is true, of course, that we can, by an
effort of the abstracting mind, conceive of an
infinite unity which alone possesses reality ; we
can, with an effort, persuade ourselves that this
infinite unity is really indivisible, and that the
world of distinctions and relations in which we
normally live is purely illusory. It is true that
we can, again with an effort, relegate time and
motion to the sphere of illusion, regarding them
as our own peculiarly inadequate apprehensions
of another dimension of unique and immovable
space. It is also true that, in certain circumstances, we can actually *feel*, as a direct intuition,
the existence of the all-comprehending unity,
can intimately realize in a single flash of insight
the illusoriness of the quotidian world of distinctions and relations. But these apocalypses
are rare, and the purely intellectual realization
of what such occasional mystical states directly
reveal can only be achieved with effort and in
the teeth of all our most fundamental habits of
thought and feeling and sensation. And even
if it were not so difficult to arrive at the vision of
what philosophers and mystics assure us, for
reasons, however, which can never be wholly
convincing, to be the Truth ; even if it were easy
for us to pass in the spirit from the world of distinctions and relations to that of infinity and
unity,—we should be no nearer to being able to

*live* in that higher world. For we live with our bodies ; and our bodies grossly refuse to be anything but distinct and relative. Nothing can induce the body to admit its own illusoriness. ' You don't really exist,' argues the intellect, poking the body in the ribs. ' You 're not there at all ; you 're just a hole in the infinite substance. There is no reality but the One.' ' With which,' adds the spirit, ' I have made a personal and ecstatic acquaintance.' ' What you regard as your substantial individuality,' the intellect goes on, ' is merely a negation of the higher reality. *Sub specie aeternitatis* your being is simply a not-being.' The body makes no reply ; but a faint rumbling in that part of the corporeal illusion which we have made a habit of calling the belly proclaims that it is more than time for lunch.

' Do what you will, this world 's a fiction.'

All the labours of all the metaphysicians who have ever thought about the Theory of Knowledge are summed up in Blake's one doggerel line. This world, the world of Spinoza's tiny worms, is unescapably a fiction. But it is no less unescapably *our* world. ' Do what we will,' we cannot get away from the fiction. It is only on rare occasions and with the greatest difficulty that we can even take a temporary holiday from the fiction—and then it is only a part of us, only the mind, that wings its way towards Reality (if indeed it *is* Reality that it flies to ; and there is, of course, no possible guarantee of that). The body, meanwhile, sits solidly among the too too solid illusions of the world, and rumbles, with what a vulgar insistence, what low and un-Platonic sounds ! wamblingly rumbles for its dinner.

Since, then, we cannot ever escape from the world of illusion, let us try to make the best of it. Necessities can be turned into excellent virtues. Fate has decreed that we shall be worms ; so let us resign ourselves to being worms ; nay, let us do more than resign ourselves, let us be worms with gusto, strenuously ; let us make up our minds to be the best of all possible worms. For, after all, a good worm is better than that nondescript creature we become when we try to live above our station, in the world of wings. No amount of trying can convert a worm into even the worst of butterflies. Ambitious to transform himself into a Swallowtail or a Camber-well Beauty, the high-minded worm does his best and in due course becomes, not even a Cabbage White, but only an inferior, half-dead version of his old self, bombinating on wings of imagination in a void. In their search for superhuman wisdom, philosophers and mystics sacrifice much valuable human knowledge, without, however, being rewarded for their sacrifice by any angelic power. What is true in the sphere of knowledge is no less true in the sphere of conduct. Burns's

Unco Guid sacrifice their humanity for the sake of achieving superhumanity. But they can never, in the nature of things, completely realize their ambition ; a part of them must always and necessarily remain on the human plane. And on this human plane their sacrifices are mutilations. In certain respects they may succeed in being, morally, more than men, but in others they become less. They mutilate themselves into subhumanity.

Since the triumph of Christianity, life in the West has been organized on the assumption that worms ought to try to become butterflies, and that, in certain circumstances, the transformation is actually possible. The attainment of more than human knowledge and a standard of more than human conduct is held up as an ideal ; and at the same time it is affirmed, or at least it is piously hoped, that this ideal is realizable. In point of fact, however, it isn't—as every one knows who has ever read a little history or biography, or has observantly frequented his fellow-creatures.

Is an ideal any the worse for being unrealizable? Many people would say that it was actually the better for it. Hang a carrot just out of the donkey's reach and he will start to run, he will go on running. But if ever he got his teeth into it, he would stop at once. It is the same, the moralists argue, with ideals ; they must be made to retire, like the carrot, as we pursue. An

easily realizable ideal quickly loses its power of
stimulation. Nothing lets a man down with
such a bump into listless disillusionment as the
discovery that he has achieved all his ambitions
and realized all his ideals. Once actually seized,
the carrot too often turns out to be a Dead Sea
fruit. Self-made men, whose ideal, when they
set out, was success, generally find themselves
compelled, when they have become successful,
to hang out other and remoter carrots in exchange
for that which they are now crunching to ashes
between their teeth. They have to pretend that
their efforts are somehow rendering a Christian
service to humanity, or that they are working for
some cause (even if it is only the cause of their
shareholders). But for these more distant and
unattainable goals they would find themselves
unable to continue their already accomplished
work of money-making. There is no possibility
of any one realizing the Christian ideals. For
human beings simply cannot, in the nature of
things, be superhuman. Those who accept these
ideals run no risk of finding themselves let down
into disillusionment and apathy. The carrot is
luscious-looking enough to start them off and
distant enough to keep them trotting for the
whole of their natural existence. So far so good.
The end proposed by the Christian ideal is attractive, its power to stimulate inexhaustible. But
if the means to that end are bad, then the power
to go on stimulating indefinitely will be a power

to go on indefinitely doing mischief. And as we have already seen, the means *are* bad. For, according to the Christian notion, superhumanness, whether of knowledge or of conduct, can only be realized through a system of morality that imposes the unremitting sacrifice of what may be called the all too human elements in human nature. But on that all too human plane, on which destiny has decreed that we shall mostly live, whether we like it or not, these sacrifices are mutilations. Those who take the Christian ideal seriously are compelled incessantly to commit a partial suicide. Luckily, the majority of nominal Christians has at no time taken the Christian ideal very seriously ; if it had, the races and the civilization of the West would long ago have come to an end. But men have taken the Christian ideal and its inferior modern successors, the scientific and the social ideals, seriously enough to inflict on themselves individually, and so, indirectly, on the civilization of which they are representatives, an injury that grows worse with the passage of time, and that, unhealed, must infallibly prove mortal.

The perfect ideal, it is obvious, is one possessing all the attractiveness and the inexhaustible stimulating power of the Christian ideal without its attendant harmfulness. Like the Christian ideal of superhumanness, it must be impossible of final realization. But the means by which men try to realize it must be such as will inflict no injury on those who use them. Such an ideal, it seems to me, would be the ideal, not of superhumanness, but of perfected humanity. Let the worm try to be superlatively himself, the best of all possible worms.

Humanity perfected and consummate—it is a high and finally unattainable ideal ; an ideal, it seems to me, superior in many ways to the Christian ideal of superhumanness. For at the root of this aspiration to be more than human in knowledge and behaviour we find, at a last analysis, a kind of cowardice, a refusal to cope, except desperately, by the most brutal and mechanical means, with the facts, the complicated difficult facts, of life. For what is the aspiration towards more than human knowledge but a flight from the infinite complexities and varieties of appearances ? The ideas of Plato, the One of Plotinus, the Alls, the Nothings, the Gods, the Infinites, the Natures of all the mystics of whatever religions, of all the transcendental philosophers, all the pantheists—what are they but convenient and consoling substitutes for the welter of immediate experience, home-made and therefore home-like spiritual snuggeries in the alien universe ? And the stoic's brutal sacrifice of the physical, instinctive and passional life, the ascetic's self-castration, the modern efficiency-monger's deprecation of all but willed and intelligent activities on the one hand, and all but purely mechanical routineering activities on the other—what are these ' high moralities' but terrified flights from the problems of social and individual life ? Harmonious living is a matter of tact and sensitiveness, of judgment and balance and incessant adjustment, of being well bred and aristocratically moral by habit and instinct. But this is too difficult. It is easier to live by fixed rules than by tact and judgment ; surgical operations are simpler than living adjustments. A cast-iron morality is not admirable ; on the contrary, it is the confession of a fear of life, of an inability to deal with the facts of experience as they present themselves—the confession, in a word, of a weakness of which men should be ashamed, not proud. To aspire to be superhuman is a most discreditable admission that you lack the guts, the wit, the moderating judgment to be successfully and consummately human.

The superhumanists are in the habit of consoling themselves for their failure to realize their ideal in the here and now by retiring into a world of fancy. Our fathers thought of this world as situated in an earthly past and also in a posthumous eternity ; the major prophets of our own day attribute to their consolatory fancies a local habitation on our own planet and in future time. This modern habit of dreaming about the imaginary future is acclaimed as a sign of our superiority to our superstitious and backward-looking ancestors. Why, goodness only knows. The most aspiring of our superhumanists is Mr.

Bernard Shaw, who invites us, in *Back to Methuse-lah*, to share his raptures at the spectacle of a future Earth inhabited by sexless old monsters of mental and physical deformity. As usual, the highest turns out in a strange way to be the lowest. We aspire in circles, and when we imagine that we are most superhuman we suddenly find ourselves below the beasts. Mr. Shaw's earthly paradise turns out to be a charnel-house. Under the galvanic stimulation of his wit the mummies frisk about like so many putrefied lambs ; it is all very amusing, no doubt, but oh, how gruesome, how unspeakably horrible ! All Mr. Shaw's writing is dry and chilly, lifeless for all its appearance of twitching liveliness. In *Back to Methuselah* the bony rattling, the crackling disintegration of the mummied tissues are deafeningly loud. Inevitably ; for *Back to Methuselah* is the most loftily idealistic, the most super-humanistic of all Mr. Shaw's plays. The highest is the lowest.

My own feeling, whenever I see a book about the Future, is one of boredom and exasperation. What on earth is the point of troubling one's head with speculations about what men may, but almost certainly will not, be like in A.D. 20,000 ? The hypothetical superman can really be left to look after himself. Since he is, by definition, essentially different from man, it is obvious that we can do nothing to accelerate or retard his coming. The only thing in our power is to do our best to be men, here and now. Let us think about the present, not the future. If we don't, there will very soon be no future to think about. Reduced by the very loftiness of their ambitions to a state of subhumanity, the aspiring supermen will have destroyed one another like so many mad dogs. Non-existence is futureless.

The means by which men try to turn themselves into supermen are murderous. The great merit of the ideal of perfected humanity is that the realization of it can only be essayed by means that are life-giving, not life-destroying. For the perfected man is the complete man, the man in whom all the elements of human nature have been developed to the highest pitch compatible with the making and holding of a psychological harmony within the individual and an external social harmony between the individual and his fellows. The surgical-operation type of morality, which is the practical complement of the super-human ideal, gives place, among those whose ambition it is to be consummately men, to a morality of living adjustments, of tact and taste, of balanced contradictions. The ideal of consummate humanity demands of those who accept it, not self-murder, but self-harmony.

The prime mistake of Christian moralists and idealists has been to suppose that the human character is fundamentally consistent ; or alternatively that, if it isn't in fact very consistent, it ought to be made so. As a matter of observable

fact, human beings are fundamentally inconsistent.
Men and women are seldom the same for more
than a few hours or even a few minutes at a
stretch. The soul is a kind of hydra—many as
well as one, numerous in its uniqueness. A man
is now one and now another of the hydra-heads
within him. Such are the obvious facts of our
daily experience. The High Moralists sometimes
deny these obvious facts, or else admit their
existence only to declare war on them. Man's
true self, they assert, is the mental self ; the rest
is illusory, accidental, unessential. These statements of fact are, of course, merely veiled expressions of desire, words of command in fancy dress.
The indicative tense is really an imperative.
When philosophers or moralists or theologians
talk about ' true ' selves, ' true ' Gods, ' true ' as
opposed to false virtues, doctrines, loves, and so
forth, all they are doing is to express their own
personal preferences. And conversely, words
like ' accidental,' ' non-essential,' ' illusory,' are
generally no more than the bad language of
learned and pious men. Their position, their
age, their cloth does not permit them to call their
opponents bloody bastards, stinkers, or swine ;
they have to content themselves with more
cumbrous and circumlocutory forms of abuse.
Those, then, who deny the facts of human nature
are only saying in a different and rather less
honest way the same thing as those who admit
but condemn them. Man is not consistent, but

he ought to be made so. For consistency, the consistency of unflagging spirituality, is one of the principal characteristics of that superhuman being that it is man's duty to become. The soul must be reduced to singleness, violently—if necessary, surgically ; all but one of the hydra's heads must be chopped off. So commands the superhumanist. The humanist, on the other hand, admits the equal right to existence of all the heads ; his preoccupation is to keep the whole collection, if not at peace (for that would be impossible), at least in a condition of balanced hostility, of chronically indecisive warfare, in which the defeats are alternate and the victories impermanent.

The humanist's system of morality is a consecration of the actual facts of life as men live it. He proceeds in the reverse direction from that taken by the superhumanist ; for, instead of passing from the arbitrary imperative to the correspondingly fantastic indicative, he moves from the indicative of the observed and experienced facts to the imperative of a realistic morality and a rational legislation.

'Homer was wrong,' wrote Heracleitus of Ephesus, ' Homer was wrong in saying : " Would that strife might perish from among gods and men ! " He did not see that he was praying for the destruction of the universe ; for if his prayer were heard, all things would pass away.' These are words which the superhumanists should meditate. Aspiring towards a consistent perfection, they are aspiring towards annihilation. The Hindus had the wit to see and the courage to proclaim the fact ; Nirvana, the goal of their striving, is nothingness. Wherever life exists, there also is inconsistency, division, strife. They are conspicuous even in the societies and individuals that accept the superhumanist ideal and are governed by the superhumanist ethic. Happily, as I have remarked before, this ideal has seldom been taken very seriously ; very few people have gone so far as to annihilate themselves completely in the attempt to realize it. Almost all the superhumanists pursue their ideal by fits and starts, and only spasmodically obey the precepts of their ethic ; in the intervals they live humanly or, more often, subhumanly ; for the higher they go in their efforts to be overmen, the lower they sink, when the efforts are relaxed, towards a repulsive subhumanity. Até and Nemesis are real beings ; their activities are daily observable. They are not, perhaps, quite so malignantly bent on punishing people who accidentally marry their mothers as the Greek tragedians seem to have supposed. Fate, in their tragedies, too often degenerates from an inner organic necessity to an external mechanical one. Certain actions are conventionally bad ; certain penalties are attached to them. Wittingly or unwittingly, a man commits one of these actions. Flop ! like a booby-trap, the suspended

penalty comes down on his head. It is all very
neat and mechanical, like a piece of the best
clockwork ; but it is not very real, it has nothing
much to do with life. We laugh at the epigram-
matist Meleager for telling the coy young Poly-
xenides to remember that time flies and that
Nemesis, in the shape of uncomely age, will soon
take vengeance on his all too smooth, his inso-
lently lovely buttocks. But the idea is really
less radically absurd than that which inspires
*Œdipus Rex.* To possess a pair of excessively
lovely buttocks, and to be vainly and coquettishly
conscious of possessing them, may easily con-
stitute a genuine offence against the golden mean.
Unwittingly to marry your mother is not a genuine outrage ; it is merely an accident. Nemesis
is the principle of equilibrium. If you don't
balance yourself, the Gods will do your balancing
for you—and do it with a vengeance ! The lives
of the most ardent superhumanists bear ample
witness to the jealousy of heaven. The *Deus
prudens*, as Horace calls the divine principle of
moderation, dislikes and punishes any exclusive
or unbalanced excess.

In practice, I repeat, the vast majority even of
superhumanists live inconsistently. They are
one thing in church and another out ; they
believe in one way and act in another ; they
temper spirituality with fleshliness, virtue with
sin, rationality with superstition. If they did not,
the races of the West would long since have

ceased to exist. Single-mindedness may save
men in the next world ; but in this there is certainly no salvation except in inconsistency. The
superhumanists have saved themselves by not
living up to their principles. But if this is so,
objects the sociologist, why seek to change their
principles ? These people survive because they
sometimes forget their principles, and they are
restrained from much socially undesirable behaviour because they sometimes live up to them.
There is no question of their beliefs being true or
false in any absolute sense of the terms. So why,
seeing that they have good social results, why
object to these beliefs ? The tree is to be judged
by its fruits and by nothing else. Agreed ; and
it is precisely because the fruits are not good
enough that I object to the tree. For though it
is true that men continue to be humanly inconsistent even under a régime that idealizes a superhuman consistency of spirituality and conscious
wilfulness, the fact of this idealization is harmful.
It is harmful because those who take the ideal
seriously (and the boldness, the very impossibility of the superhuman ambition attracts the
men and women who are potentially the best) do
vital damage not only to themselves, but also,
by their precept and example, to their fellows.
Even to those who do not take it with such a
suicidal or murderous seriousness, the superhuman ideal is harmful. Their belief is not
strong enough to prevent them from living incon-

sistently ; but it *is* strong enough to make them regard their inconsistencies as rather discreditable, to make them feel ashamed of all but one, or at most a few, out of all the hydra heads of their multifarious being. Their superhumanist morality makes them condemn as sinful, or low, or degrading, or at best trivial and unserious, the greater number of their normal activities. They do what their instincts command, but apologetically. They have remorse for their passions, and regret that their bodies are made of too too solid flesh. The result, naturally enough, is that the quality of their instinctive, passional and physical life degenerates. You cannot think badly of a thing without its becoming bad.

'All the Gods ought to have praise given to them,' says Pausanias in the *Symposium*. All—the common as well as the heavenly Aphrodite, Athena as well as Ares and Bacchus, Pan and Priapus and the Satyrs no less than Artemis, Apollo, and the Muses. In other words, all the manifestations of life are godlike, and every element of human nature has a right—a divine right, even—to exist and find expression.

That a stable society can be formed by men and women, who profess the worship of life in all its inconsistent and contradictory manifestations, is a fact that can be demonstrated out of Greek history. Pericles in his funeral oration over the first victims of the Peloponnesian War has left an admirable description of fifth-century Athens. It was a place, he said (I paraphrase and abridge), where all could freely express their opinions on affairs of state ; where all were free, in domestic matters, to do what they liked ; where nobody officiously interfered with other people's private lives, and no man's personal amusements were ever counted against him as a crime. In their private relationships the Athenians were free ; but in all that concerned the fatherland, a wholesome fear prevented them from playing false ; they obeyed the magistrates and the laws. The fatigues of public business were tempered by public entertainments and private amusements. To the worshippers of barrack-room discipline—the repulsive brood is still with us— Pericles replied with a comparison between Athenians and Spartans. The Spartans ' toil from early boyhood in a laborious pursuit after courage, while we, free to live and wander as we please, march out none the less to face the self-same dangers. If we choose to face dangers with an easy mind, rather than after rigorous training, and to trust rather in native manhood than in state-made courage, the advantage lies with us ; for we are spared all the weariness of practising for future hardships, and when we find ourselves among them we are as brave as our plodding rivals.' These were not the only titles to men's admiration that the Athenians could show. ' We are lovers of beauty without extravagance and of

79

wisdom without unmanliness. Our citizens attend to both private and public duties, and do not allow absorption in their own affairs to interfere with their knowledge of the city's.' The only defect in this description is that it is too sober, insufficiently emphatic—at any rate for us, to whom everything that Pericles took for granted is utterly foreign. How foreign, few even of those who have had a sound classical education, even of professional scholars, seem ever to realize. The unawareness is at bottom voluntary. We do not really *want* to realize the full extent of the difference between the Greek worldview, the Greek way of life, and our own. For most of us the realization would be too disturbing ; so we shut our eyes on all that would force it upon us and continue to visualize the Greeks, if we visualize them at all (which a great many very estimable scholars never do, preferring to pursue their studies in the abstract, as though the Hellenic world were nothing but a complicated series of algebraical equations), as a race of very nice, handsome, and intelligent English public-school boys. But in fact the Greeks were neither nice nor boyish. They were men—men how incomparably completer and more adult than the decayed or fossil children who, at our Universities, profess themselves the guardians of the Greek tradition ! And their behaviour, according to our standards, was very frequently outrageous and disgusting.

What Pericles took for granted was briefly this : that men should accept their natures as they found them. Man has a mind : very well, let him think. Senses that enjoy : let him be sensual. Instincts : they are there to be satisfied. Passions : it does a man good to succumb to them from time to time. Imagination, a feeling for beauty, a sense of awe : let him create, let him surround himself with lovely forms, let him worship. Man is multifarious, inconsistent, self-contradictory ; the Greeks accepted the fact and lived multifariously, inconsistently, and contradictorily. Their polytheism gave divine sanction to this realistic acceptance. 'All the Gods ought to have praise given to them.' There was therefore no need for remorse or the consciousness of sin. The preservation of the unstable equilibrium between so many mutually hostile elements was a matter of tact and common-sense and aesthetic judgment. At the same time the habits of patriotic devotion and obedience to the laws acted powerfully as a restraining and moderating force. More powerfully, perhaps, than with us. For the liberty of the Ancients was not the same as ours. So far as their private lives, their domestic relations, were concerned, it was complete ; but in regard to the state it was strictly limited. It never occurred to a Greek to claim the modern individualist's anarchic licences. As a citizen he felt that he owed himself and all he possessed to the city. This sentiment was

still strong enough, even in the last centuries of
the Roman Empire, to make it possible for the
Emperors to demand from their more prosperous
subjects the most inordinate sacrifices in money,
time, and trouble. At the beginning of the
fourth century the laborious and expensive
honours of senatorial office in the provinces were
made compulsory and hereditary. The unhappy
magistrates and all their posterity were condemned to a kind of endless penal servitude and
perpetual fine—to a hereditary punishment, of
which the only foreseeable term was either the
total extinction or else the irremediable ruin of
the family. No modern ruler could demand such
sacrifices of his subjects ; the attempt would pro-
voke an immediate revolution. The Romans
of the fourth century resigned themselves ; they
were citizens, and they knew that it was the business of the citizen to pay. That the traditions
of good citizenship are not enough of themselves
to keep the man (as opposed to the citizen) well
balanced and harmonized is demonstrated by
the history of the Romans. Devoid, as they
were, of aesthetic tact and judgment, lacking the
Greek's fine sense of proportion and harmony,
the Romans lapsed, as soon as they had made
themselves masters of the world, into a condition of the most repulsive moral squalor. Like
the Spartans, they were only virtuous in the
barrack-room.

The Greeks, then, were realists. They recognized the fact of human inconsistency and suited their religion, their morality, their social organization to it. We should do well to follow their example. Indeed, the modern circumstances make it imperative that we should raise our moral inconsistency to the rank of a principle ; for the modern circumstances are so hostile to man's multifarious life that, unless we insist on our diversity, we run the risk of being killed by them.

What are these dangers that threaten our world ? And how would the Greeks have guarded against them ?

Of monotheism and the menace of the super-humanist ideal I have already spoken. The Greeks, as I have shown, aspired to be, not supermen, but men—that is to say, multifarious creatures living in a state of balanced hostility between their component elements—and they regarded all the manifestations of life as divine.

The worship of success and efficiency constitutes another menace to our world. What our ancestors sacrificed on the altars of Spirituality, we sacrificed on those of the Bitch Goddess and Taylorism. The work of Weber, Tawney, and other contemporary historians has clearly shown the part played by the Reformation and Protestantism in the propagation of success-worship. The Protestants believed in the Bible and Predestination. Most of the Bible is about the ancient Hebrews, who did not believe in the immortality of the soul and considered that virtue was, or at any rate ought to be, rewarded in this world by an increase of this world's goods. Calvinistic predestination teaches that Grace is everything, and that works—especially those works most highly praised by mediæval theologians, such as contemplation, learning, ascetic practices, and charity—are nothing. Grace might be found as easily in the successful business man as in the contemplative ascetic. More easily, indeed. For the fact that the business man was successful proved, according to Old Testament notions, that God was on his side ; and God was on his side because he was virtuous. The disinterested, contemplative, charitable man was hopelessly unsuccessful. God, therefore, must hate him. Why ? Because he was wicked. By the beginning of the eighteenth century and in the best Protestant circles, true goodness was measured in terms of cash. Mediæval spirituality was certainly deplorable ; but still more deplorable is modern success-worship. If a man must commit partial suicide, it is better that he should do so in the name of disinterestedness, of contemplation and charity, than in that of money and comfort. Asceticism for the love of God is bad enough ; asceticism for the love of Mammon is intolerable. But it is for the love of Mammon that our modern stoics exhort us to mortify our flesh and control our passions. Thus, Big Business supports prohibition because, in Mr. Ford's words, we must choose between drink and in-

dustrialism ; because, in Mr. Gary's, drink and
prosperity are incompatible. Industrialism
would work still more efficiently, prosperity
would be even greater, if we could prohibit, not
only whisky, but also sex and science, the love
of knowledge and the love of women, creative
imagination and creative desire. Deprived of
all their distractions, shut out from all their private
paradises, men would work almost as well as
machines. The one legitimate desire left them
would be a desire for things—for all the countless
unnecessary things, the possession of which constitutes prosperity. We should be grateful to
Protestantism for having helped, entirely against
the wishes and intentions of its founders, to
emancipate the human mind. But let us not
forget to hate it for having degraded all the
ancient standards of value, for having sanctified
wealth and put a halo on the head of the Pharisee.
The Reformers pulled down the Virgin Mary,
but they stuck the Bitch Goddess in her place. I
am not, personally, a great enthusiast for virgins ;
but I prefer them, on the whole, to bitches. *Faute
de mieux*. But something better does exist. What
we need is a new Reformation, a Hellenic Reformation made by men with the sense to see that
there is a happy mean between bitchery and
virginity, that the legitimate occupant of the
shrine is neither the one nor the other, but Aphrodite or the Great Mother. The Greeks were
neither À Kempises nor Smileses. They refused

to sacrifice the body to the spirit ; but even more emphatically they refused to sacrifice both body and spirit to the Bitch Goddess.

The third of the great modern menaces to life, the root of many widely ramifying evils, is the machine. The machine is dangerous because it is not only a labour-saver, but also a creation-saver. Creative work, of however humble a kind, is the source of man's most solid, least transitory happiness. The machine robs the majority of human beings of the very possibility of this happiness. Leisure has now been almost as completely mechanized as labour. Men no longer amuse themselves, creatively, but sit and are passively amused by mechanical devices. Machinery condemns one of the most vital needs of humanity to a frustration which the progress of invention can only render more and more complete. But, though harmful, the use of machinery cannot be discontinued. Simple-lifers, like Tolstoy and Gandhi, ignore the most obvious facts. Chief among these is the fact that machinery, by increasing production, has permitted an increase of population. There are twice as many human beings to-day as there were a hundred years ago. The existence of this increased population is dependent on the existence of modern machinery. If we scrap the machinery, we kill at least half the population. When Gandhi advocates the return to handicrafts, he is advocating the condemnation to death of

about nine hundred million human beings.
Tamburlane's butcheries are insignificant compared with the cosmic massacre so earnestly
advocated by our mild and graminivorous
Mahatma. No, the slaughter of nine hundred
million human beings is not a piece of practical
politics. The machines must stay ; it is obvious.
They must stay, even though, used as they are
now being used, they inflict on humanity an
enormous psychological injury that must, if un-
cared for, prove mortal. The only remedy is
systematic inconsistency. The life-quenching
work at machine or desk must be regarded as a
necessary evil to be compensated for by the
creative labours or amusements of leisure. But
most contemporary leisures, as we have already
seen, are as completely dominated by the creation-
saving machine as most contemporary work.
Before leisure can be made to serve as an antidote
to life-destroying work it must be de-mechanized.
The task will prove by no means easy. Leisure
can only be de-mechanized if a general desire
for its de-mechanization is first created. Powerful forces oppose, from within and without, the
creation of this desire. From within come lazi-
ness and the psychological *vis inertiæ* that is the
life of habits. Men find it easier to let themselves
be passively amused than to go out and create.
True, creation is interesting and passivity profoundly boring. But even boring effortlessness
is a luxury, and a habit of idleness, however life-

destroying, is difficult to break. Passivity and subservience to machinery blunt the desire and diminish the power to create ; pursuing the ideal of superhuman business efficiency, men mutilate the imaginative and instinctive side of their natures. The result is that they lose their sense of values, their taste and judgment become corrupted, and they have an irresistible tendency to love the lowest when they see it. The lowest is copiously provided by the film-makers, the newspaper proprietors, the broadcasters, and all the rest. And though this love of the lowest is mixed with an indescribable ennui, it will resist any attempt to remove its debased and dismal object. This resistance is encouraged by those who have a financial interest in the providing of standardized creation-saving entertainments for the masses. The sums invested in the amusement industry are enormous ; creation-saving has become a vested interest of the first magnitude. If men were to take to amusing themselves instead of suffering themselves to be passively amused, millions upon millions of capital would be lost. Any attempt to do so is therefore resisted. The propaganda in favour of the creation-saving amusements is unflagging and dreadfully effective—for it is our unenviable distinction to have brought the ancient arts of lying and sophistry and persuasion to what would seem an absolute perfection. In every newspaper and magazine, from every hoarding, on the screen of every

picture-palace, the same assertions are endlessly
repeated : that there are no amusements outside
those provided by the great creation-saving
companies ; that the height of human happiness
is to sit and be passively entertained by machines,
and that those who do not submit to this process of entertainment are not merely to be pitied
as miserable, but to be despised as old-fashioned
provincial boobies. In the teeth of this propaganda it will clearly be difficult to create a
desire for the de-mechanization of leisure. But
unless such a desire is created, the races of the
industrialized West are doomed, it seems to me,
to self-destruction—to a kind of suicide while of
unsound mind. The first symptoms of mass
insanity are everywhere apparent. A few years
more, and the patient will be raving and violent.
The preaching, the organizing, the practising of
inconsistency are matters of the most rudimentary political expediency. The statesmanship of the immediate future will be concerned
(if it is good statesmanship) above all with questions of psychology—with the relations between
the individual and his surroundings, and of the
component parts of the individual with one
another. Political economy, the balance of
power, the organization of government, will
become matters of secondary importance. Inevitably; for an answered riddle ceases to perplex.
The old political riddles are not, indeed,
answered ; but they are at least showing signs

that they are answerable. Thus the problems connected with the distribution of wealth, supposed at one time to be soluble only by revolutionary methods, are now in process of being peacefully liquidated. For the capitalists have found that it pays them to keep the standard of life as high as possible. So long as the planetary resources hold out, the mass-producers will do their best to make everybody more and more prosperous. National rivalry is still a source of grave dangers ; the War to end War was concluded by a Peace most beautifully calculated to end peace. But meanwhile capitalism is becoming more and more international ; it pays Big Business to avoid War. Peace on earth and good will among men are the soundest of sound investments. If only, on the first Christmas Day, the angels had taken the trouble to tell us so ! As for the problems of government, they are not solved, and they can never be definitely solved, for the simple reason that societies change, and that the forms of government must change with them. There is no absolutely right kind of government. Men have at last come to realize this simple but important fact, with the result that, for the first time in history, the problems of government can be discussed in a relatively scientific and rational spirit. Even the divine rights of parliamentarism and political democracy can now be questioned with impunity. Ever since the world was made safe for it, democracy has steadily been losing its prestige. People feel a great deal less fanatically about Liberty, Equality, Fraternity than they did even a generation ago ; they are ready to approach the problem of government in almost the same detached and irreligious spirit as that in which they now approach the exactly analogous problem of repairing the radio set or building a house. To have adopted this attitude towards the problem is to have gone half-way towards its solution.

No, the old political issues have receded into relative unimportance. The vital problem of our age is the problem of reconciling manhood with the citizenship of a modern industrialized state. The modern Good Citizen, who is nothing more than a Good Citizen, is less than human, an imbecile or a lunatic—dangerous to himself and to the society in which he lives. In the existing industrial circumstances he can only be a man out of business hours. He must live two lives—or rather one life and one automatic simulation of life. Religion, philosophy, politics, and ethics must conspire to impose on him a double inconsistency—as between man and citizen in the first place, and, in the second, as between the various component elements of the man. The present attempt to impose a superhuman consistency whether of spirituality, of intellect, of mechanical efficiency, results in the imposition of subhuman insanity. From madness in the long-run comes destruction. It is only by cultivating his humanity that man can hope to save himself. The difficulties of the task, as we have seen, are enormously great. But so are the penalties of failure. Spinoza's little worm has the choice of desperately attempting to remain a little worm, or of ceasing to exist.

'The Queen,' writes Swift in one of his letters to Stella, ' the Queen is well, but I fear she will be no long liver ; for I am told she has sometimes the gout in her bowels (I hate the word bowels).' Yes, how he hated it ! And not the word only—the things too, the harmless neces- sary tripes—he loathed and detested them with an intensity of hatred such as few men have ever been capable of. It was unbearable to him that men should go through life with guts and sweet- breads, with livers and lights, spleens and kidneys. That human beings should have to get rid of the waste products of metabolism and digestion was for Swift a source of excruciating suffering. And if the Yahoos were all his personal enemies, that was chiefly because they smelt of sweat and excrement, because they had genital organs and dugs, groins and hairy armpits ; their moral shortcomings were of secondary importance. Swift's poems about women are more ferocious even than his prose about 'the Yahoos ; his resentment against women for being warm- blooded mammifers was incredibly bitter. Read (with a bottle of smelling-salts handy, if you happen to be delicately stomached) ' The Lady's Dressing-Room,' ' Cassinus and Peter,' ' A Beautiful Young Nymph going to Bed.' Here is a moderately characteristic sample :

> And first a dirty smock appeared,
> Beneath the armpits well besmeared . . .
> But oh ! it turned poor Stephen's bowels,
> When he beheld and smelt the towels,
> Begummed, besmattered, and beslimed,
> With dirt and sweat and earwax grimed.

Passing from description to philosophical reflection, we find such lines as these :

> His foul imagination links
> Each dame he sees with all her stinks ;
> And if unsavoury odours fly,
> Conceives a lady standing by.

Nor can I refrain from mentioning that line, which Swift thought so much of that he made it the culmination of two several poems :

> Oh, Celia, Celia, Celia . . . !

The monosyllabic verb, which the modesties of 1929 will not allow me to reprint, rhymes with ' wits ' and ' fits.'

Swift must have ' hated the word bowels ' to the verge of insanity : nothing short of the most violent love or the intensest loathing could possibly account for so obsessive a preoccupation with the visceral and excrementitious subject. Most of us dislike bad smells and offal ; but so mildly that, unless they are actually forced upon our senses, we seldom think of them. Swift hated bowels with such a passionate abhorrence that he felt a perverse compulsion to bathe continually in the squelchy imagination of them. Human beings are always fascinated by what horrifies and disgusts them. The reasons are obscure and doubtless complicated. One of the sources of this apparent perversity is surely to be found in the almost universal craving for excitement. Life, for most people, is a monotonous affair ; they want to be thrilled, stimulated, excited, almost at all costs. The horrifying and disgusting are sources of strong emotion ; therefore the horrifying and disgusting are pursued as goods. Most of us, I suppose, enjoy disgust and horror, at any rate in small doses. But we fairly quickly reach a point where the enjoyment turns into pain ; when this happens we naturally do our best to avoid the source of the painful emotions. But there are at least two classes of people who are ready voluntarily to continue the pursuit of horrors and disgustfulnesses long after the majority of their fellows have begun to shrink from a pleasure which has become an intolerable pain. In the first class we find the congenitally insensitive—those who can be excited only by a relatively enormous stimulus. The extreme case is that of certain idiots for whom a surgical operation without anaesthetics is a real pleasure. Under the knife and the cautery they begin at last to feel. Between this extreme of insensitiveness and the statistical normal there is no hiatus, but a continuous series of graded types, for all of whom the normal stimulus is to a greater or less degree inadequate. To the congenitally insensitive we must add those whose normal sensitiveness has, for one reason or another, decreased during the course of life. A familiar type is that of the ageing debauchee, habituated to a continuous excitement, but so much exhausted by his mode of life, so blunted and hardened, that he can only be excited by a more than normally powerful stimulus. Such insensitives can stomach doses of horror and disgust which would be mortal to the ordinary man.

But the insensitives are not the only lovers of horror and disgust. There is another class of men and women, often more than ordinarily sensitive, who deliberately seek out what pains and nauseates them for the sake of the extraordinary pleasure they derive from the overcoming of their repulsion. Take the case, for example, of the mystical Mme. Guyon, who felt that her repugnance for unclean and unsavoury objects was a weakness disgraceful in one who lived only for and with God. One day she determined to overcome this weakness, and, seeing on the ground a particularly revolting gob of phlegm and spittle, she picked it up and, in spite of intolerable retchings of disgust, put it in her mouth. Her nauseated horror was succeeded by a sentiment of joy, of profound exultation. A similar incident may be found in the biography of St. Francis of Assisi. Almost the first act of his religious life was to kiss the pustulent hand of one of those lepers, the sight and smell of whom had, up till that time, sickened him with disgust. Like Mme. Guyon, he was rewarded for his pains with a feeling of rapturous happiness. Even the most unsaintly people have felt the glow of satisfaction which follows the accomplishment of some act in the teeth of an instinctive resistance. The pleasure of asserting the conscious will against one of those dark instinctive forces which consciousness rightly regards as its enemies, is for many people, and in certain circumstances, more than sufficient to outweigh the pain caused by the thwarting of the instinct. Our minds, like our bodies, are colonies of separate lives, existing in a state of chronically hostile symbiosis ; the soul is in reality a great conglomeration of souls, the product of whose endless warfare at any given moment is our behaviour at that moment. The pleasures attending the victory of conscious will have a special quality of their own, a quality which, for many temperaments, makes them preferable to any other kind of pleasure. Nietzsche advised men to be cruel to themselves, not because asceticism was pleasing to some hypothetical god, but because it was a good spiritual exercise, because it wound up the will and enhanced the sense of power and of conscious, voluntary life. To this delightful enhancement of the sense of power the believer, whose conscious will is fighting for what is imagined to be an absolute good, can add the no less delightful sense of being virtuous, the pleasing

consciousness that he is pleasing God. Mme.
Guyon and St. Francis probably did not ex-
aggerate when they described in such rapturous
terms the joy evoked in them by their voluntary
wallowings in filth.

Swift—to return from a long digression—Swift
belonged, it seems to me, to a sub-species of the
second category of horror-lovers. He was not
one of those insensitives who can only respond
to the most violent stimuli. On the contrary, he
seems to have been more than normally sensitive.
His 'hatred of bowels' was the rationalization
of an intense disgust. Why, then, did he pore
so lingeringly on what revolted him ? What was
his reward ? Was it the Nietzschean enhancement of the sense of power ? Or was it the
Christian's happy consciousness of pleasing God
by the conquest of a weakness ? No, it was
certainly not for the love of God that the Dean of
St. Patrick's humiliated himself in the excrement
and offal. Was it, then, for love of himself, for
the pleasure of asserting his will ? A little,
perhaps. But his real reward was the pain he
suffered. He felt a compulsion to remind himself of his hatred of bowels, just as a man with a
wound or an aching tooth feels a compulsion to
touch the source of his pain—to make sure that it
is still there and still agonizing. With Swift, it
was not a case of the pleasure of self-assertion out-
weighing the pain of voluntarily-evoked disgust.
For him the pain *was* the pleasure, or, at any

rate, it was the desirable end towards which his activities were directed. He wished to suffer.

Swift's greatness lies in the intensity, the almost insane violence of that ' hatred of bowels ' which is the essence of his misanthropy and which underlies the whole of his work. As a doctrine, a philosophy of life, this misanthropy is profoundly silly. Like Shelley's apocalyptic philanthropy, it is a protest against reality, childish (for it is only the child who refuses to accept the order of things), like all such protests, from the fairy story to the socialist's Utopia. Regarded as a political pamphlet or the expression of a world-view, *Gulliver* is as preposterous as *Prometheus Unbound*. Regarded as works of art, as independent universes of discourse existing on their own authority, like geometries harmoniously developed from a set of arbitrarily chosen axioms, they are almost equally admirable. What interests me here, however, is the relation of these two works to the reality outside themselves, not the inward, formal relation of their component parts with one another. Considered, then, merely as comments on reality, *Gulliver* and *Prometheus* are seen, for all their astonishing difference, to have a common origin—the refusal on the part of their authors to accept the physical reality of the world. Shelley's refusal to accept the given reality took the form of a lyrical and prophetic escape into the Golden Age that is to be when kings and priests have been destroyed and the worship of

abstractions and metaphysical absolutes is substituted for that of the existing gods. Swift, on
the contrary, made no attempt to escape, but
remained earth-bound, rubbing his nose in all
those aspects of physical reality which most
distressed him. His Houyhnhnm Utopia was
not one of those artificial paradises which men
have fabricated (out of such diverse materials as
religious myths, novels, and whisky) as a refuge
from a world with which they were unable to
cope. He was not like that Old Person of Bazing
in Edward Lear's rhyme, who

> purchased a steed
> Which he rode at full speed
> To escape from the people of Bazing.

Swift's horse was not a means of transport into
another and better world. A winged angel
would have served that purpose better. If he
' purchased a steed,' it was in order that he might
shame the disgusting Yahoos by parading its
superiority. For Swift, the charm of the country
of the Houhynhnms consisted, not in the beauty
and virtue of the horses, but in the foulness of the
degraded men.

When we look into the matter we find that the
great, the unforgivable sin of the Yahoos consisted in the fact that they possessed bowels. Like
so many of the Fathers of the Church, Swift could
not forgive men and women for being vertebrate
mammals as well as immortal souls. He could

not forgive them, in a word, for actually existing.
It is unnecessary for me to insist at length on the
absurdity, the childish silliness, of this refusal to
accept the universe as it is given. Abstractions
are made from reality and labelled soul, spirit,
and so forth ; reality is then hated for not resembling these arbitrary abstractions from its
total mass. It would be as sensible to hate flowers
for not resembling the liquid perfume which can
be distilled from them. A yet greater, but no
less common, childishness is to hate reality because
it does not resemble the fairy stories which men
have invented to console themselves for the dis-
comforts and difficulties of daily life, or to hate it
because life does not seem to hold the significance
which a favourite author happens to have attributed to it. Ivan Karamazov returning God his
entrance ticket to life is a characteristic example
of this last form of childishness. Ivan is distressed because the real universe bears so little
resemblance to the providential machine of
Christian theology, distressed because he can
find no meaning or purpose in life. But the
purpose of life, outside the mere continuance of
living (already a most noble and beautiful end),
is the purpose we put into it : its meaning is
whatever we may choose to call the meaning.
Life is not a cross-word puzzle, with an answer
settled in advance and a prize for the ingenious
person who noses it out. The riddle of the universe has as many answers as the universe has

living inhabitants. Each answer is a working hypothesis, in terms of which the answerer experiments with reality. The best answers are those which permit the answerer to live most fully, the worst are those which condemn him to partial or complete death. The most fantastic answers will serve their turn as working hypotheses. Thus, certain primitive peoples are convinced that they are blood brothers to crocodiles or parrots, and live in accordance with their belief —most efficiently, according to all accounts. We smile at their philosophy. But is it more ridiculous, after all, than that which teaches that men are brothers, not to parrots, but to imaginary angels ? Or that an abstraction called the soul is the essential reality of human nature, and the body is hardly more than an accident, an evil accident at that ?

Of the possible reasons for Swift's insensate hatred of bowels I will say more later. It was a hatred to which, of course, he had a perfect right. Every man has an inalienable right to the psychological major premiss of his philosophy of life, just as every man has an alienable right to his own liver. But his liver may be a bad liver : it may make him sluggish, ill-tempered, despairingly melancholy. It may, in a word, be a hindrance to living instead of a help. It is the same with a philosophy of life. Every man has a right to look at the world as he chooses ; but his world-view may be a bad one—a hindrance,

like the defective liver, instead of a help to living.
Judged by these standards, the Swiftian world-
view is obviously bad. To hate bowels, to hate
the body and all its ways, as Swift hated them,
is to hate at least half of man's entire vital activity.
It is impossible to live completely without accepting life as a whole in all its manifestations.
Swift's prodigious powers were marshalled on
the side of death, not life. How instructive, in
this context, is the comparison with Rabelais !
Both men were scatological writers. Mass for
mass, there is probably more dung and offal
piled up in Rabelais' work than in Swift's. But
how pleasant is the dung through which Gargantua wades, how almost delectable the offal !
The muck is transfigured by love ; for Rabelais
loved the bowels which Swift so malignantly
hated. His was the true *amor fati* : he accepted
reality in its entirety, accepted with gratitude
and delight this amazingly improbable world,
where flowers spring from manure, and reverent
Fathers of the Church, as in Harington's *Meta-
morphosis of Ajax*, meditate on the divine mysteries
while seated on the privy ; where the singers of
the most mystically spiritual love, such as Dante,
Petrarch, and Cavalcanti, have wives and rows
of children ; and where the violences of animal
passion can give birth to sentiments of the most
exquisite tenderness and refinement. In this
most beautiful, ridiculous, and tragic world
Swift has no part : he is shut out from it by

hatred, by his childish resentment against reality
for not being entirely different from what, in
fact, it is. That the lovely Celia should obey the
calls of nature like any cow or camel, is for Swift
a real disaster. The wise and scientific Rabe-
laisian, on the other hand, would be distressed
if she did not obey them, would prescribe a visit
to Carlsbad or Montecatini. Swift would have
liked Celia to be as bodiless as an abstraction :
he was furious with her for being solid and healthy.
One is amazed that a grown man should feel and
think in a manner so essentially childish. That
the hatred of bowels should have been the major
premiss of his philosophy when Swift was fifteen
is comprehensible, but that it should have
remained the major premiss when he was forty
requires some explanation.

At this distance of time and with only the most
inadequate evidence on which to go, we cannot
hope to explain with certainty : the best we can
do is to hazard a guess, to suggest a possible
hypothesis. That which I would suggest—and
doubtless it has been suggested before—is that
Swift's hatred of bowels was obscurely, but none
the less closely, connected with that ' temperamental coldness ' which Sir Leslie Stephen
attributes to the mysterious lover of Stella and
Vanessa. That any man with a normal dosage
of sexuality could have behaved quite so oddly
as Swift behaved towards the women he loved
seems certainly unlikely. We are almost forced

by the surviving evidence to believe that some physical or psychological impediment debarred him from making love in the ordinary, the all too human manner. Now, when a man is not actually, or at any rate potentially, all too human, he does not for that reason become superhuman : on the contrary, he tends to become subhuman. Subhumanly silly, as Kant was silly in the intervals of writing the superhuman *Critique of Pure Reason* ; or subhumanly malignant, as the too virtuous Calvin was malignant. Cut off by some accident of body or character from the beautiful and humorous, the rather absurd but sacred, but sublime and marvellous world of carnal passion and tenderness (and lacking the aid of the flesh, the spirit must remain for ever ignorant of the highest, the profoundest, the intensest forms of love), Swift was prevented from growing to full human maturity. Remaining subhumanly childish, he continued all his life to resent reality for not resembling the abstractions and fairy-tale compensations of the philosophers and theologians. At the same time his separation from the human world, his sense of solitude, developed in him something of the subhuman malignity, the hate, the envious ' righteous indignation ' of the Puritan. The reverse of this ferocious hater was, as so often happens, a sentimentalist—a sentimentalist, moreover, of the worst kind ; for, in the writer of the baby-language which fills so much space

in Swift's *Journal to Stella,* we see that most
abject and repulsive type of sentimentalist (a
type, it may be added, exceedingly common at
the present time), the adult man who deliberately
mimics the attitudes of childhood. The character of the age in which Swift lived was hard
and virile : machinery, Taylorization, the highly-
organized division of labour, specialization, and
humanitarianism had not yet begun to produce
their dehumanizing effects. In the England of
the early seventeen-hundreds, Swift was ashamed
of his infantility. His baby-language was a
secret between himself and the two 'sweet
rogues' to whom he wrote his letters. In public
he revealed only the Puritan, the Father-of-the-
Church side of him—the respectably misan-
thropical obverse of the infantile medal. If he
had lived two hundred years later in our routine-
ridden, mechanized world of flabbily subhuman
sentimentalists, he would not have been ashamed
of his infantility : on the contrary, he would
have been proud. His angers and his hatreds
are what he would have hidden from the modern
public. If Swift were alive to-day, he would be
the adored, the baroneted, the Order-of-Merited
author, not of *Gulliver,* not of *The Tale of a Tub,*
not of the *Advice to Servants,* not of *The Lady's
Dressing-Room,* but of *A Kiss for Cinderella* and
*Peter Pan.*

# PARADISE

Between the road and the sea a grove of palms bore unimpeachable witness to the mildness of the climate. Exotic—their leaves a plume of gigantic parrot's feathers, each trunk an elephant's hind leg—they guaranteed us against all Northern inclemencies. The vegetable cannot lie. Or so one obstinately goes on believing, in spite of the bananas that almost ripen at Penzance, the bamboos that wave in the March wind, as though Surrey were the Malay Peninsula. ' No deception, ladies and gentlemen,' the palm-trees seemed to say. And, indeed, that was what they were there to say : what an astute town council, when it planted them, had intended them to say, ' No deception. The climate of the Mediterranean is genuinely sub-tropical.' After a bout of influenza, sub-tropicality was just what I needed : was what, so far, I had been looking for in vain. We had driven all day along a rain-blurred, wind-buffeted Riviera. A cold, fatiguing journey that might have been through Scotland. But now the gale had dropped, the evening was crystalline. Those palm-trees in the level sunlight were like a Bible picture of the Promised Land. And the hotel that looked out over their green tops to the sea was called the Hôtel Paradiso. That settled it. We decided to stop—for weeks, if necessary ; till I felt perfectly well again.

Paradise began by giving us a surprise. One does not expect to find, in the hall of an Italian hotel, a group of middle-aged English ladies dressed as female Pierrots, geishas, and Welsh peasants. But there they were, when we went to inquire about rooms, high hats, kimonos and all, chatting in the most animated manner with a young clergyman, whose clerical-Oxonian accent ('he that hath eeyars to heeyar, let him heeyar') and whose laughter (that too too merry laughter of clergymen who want to prove that, *malgré tout*, they can be good fellows) were a joy to hear.

A handbill posted on the porter's desk explained the mystery. Somewhat belatedly—for Lent was already ten days old—the town was celebrating Carnival. We read, in that magniloquent Italian style, of grandiose processions, allegorical cars, huge prizes for the best costumes, sportive manifestations in the shape of bicycle races, masked balls. The geishas and the Welsh colleens (or are they something else in Wales?) were immediately accounted for. And perhaps, I thought for a moment, perhaps the clergyman was also a masker. The stage curate is an old favourite. But listening again to the voice, the merry, merry laughter, I knew that no sacrilege had been committed. The sable uniform was certainly not a fancy dress.

Before dinner we took a stroll through the town —only to discover that the town did not exist.

True, there were houses enough, hundreds of
white stucco boxes, all very new and neat.
Bricks and mortar in plenty, but no people.
The houses were all shuttered and empty. In
summer, during the bathing season, they would
doubtless be tenanted. The town would come
to life. But at this season it was a corpse. We
looked for the *centro della città* ; in vain, the city
had no centre. The only shop we saw was an
English tea-room. In the main street we met a
wagon draped in red and yellow bunting. Very
slowly, a hearse in motley, it rolled along behind
two aged horses ; and a little crowd of twenty
or thirty men and boys, somewhat the worse for
wine, straggled after it, lugubriously singing.
They were, I suppose, the natives, making merry
behind one of Carnival's allegorical cars. We
hurried back to Paradise. The colleen and the
geisha were still talking with the clergyman. In
the background a group of old ladies muttered
over their knitting.

Hungry after a long day's journey, we responded punctually to the dinner-bell. A few
of the tables were already occupied. Isolated
in the middle of the dining-room, a little old
woman in black was eating earnestly, almost
with passion—the passionate greed of one whom
age and circumstances had deprived of every
other outlet for the libido. In a distant corner
two manifest spinsters of forty-five were engaged
with their soup. They wore semi-evening

dresses, and when they moved there was a dim glitter of semi-precious stones, a dry rattling of beads. Their hair was light, almost colourless, and frizzy with much curling. We began our meal. Two more old ladies came in, a cadaver and a black satin balloon. A mother, widowed, with three daughters who had been pretty a few years ago and were now fading, had faded already into a definite unmarriageableness, sat down at the table next to ours. An artistic lady followed. Her sage-green dress was only semi-semi-evening, and the beads she wore were definitely non-precious. Another widowed mother with an unmarried daughter who had never been pretty at any time. Another solitary old lady. The parson and his wife—what a relief to see a pair of trousers! An old lady who hobbled in with the help of a stick and a companion. The stick was of ebony; the companion had the white opaque complexion of a plucked chicken.

In a few minutes all the tables were occupied. There were, perhaps, forty guests—all English, and all, except the parson and myself, women. And what women! We looked at one another and would have laughed, if the spectacle of so much age and virtue and ugliness, so much frustration and refinement, so much middle-class pride on such small fixed incomes, so much ennui and self-sacrifice, had not been painfully distressing as well as grotesque. And suddenly it occurred to me that the whole Riviera, from

Marseilles to Spezia, was teeming with such women. In a single appalling intuition I realized all their existences. At that very moment, I reflected, in all the cheap hotels and pensions of the Mediterranean littoral, thousands upon thousands of them were eating their fish with that excessive middle-class refinement which makes one long, in the Maison Lyons, for the loud bad manners of provincial France or Belgium. Thousands upon thousands of them, trying to keep warm, trying to keep well through the winter, trying to find in foreign parts distraction and novelty and cheapness. But the wind howls in spite of the palm-trees. The rain comes lashing down. The little towns on their bays between the rocky headlands are utterly dead. The only distraction is the chat of other women of their kind. The only novelties are the latest things in semi-evening dresses and semi-precious beads. The franc and the lira never buy as much as one expects. Income remains irrevocably fixed—and so do morals and intellectual interests, so do prejudices, manners, and habits.

In the lounge, waiting for the coffee, we got into conversation with the clergyman. Or rather, he got into conversation with us. He felt it his duty, I suppose, as a Christian, as a temporary chaplain in the Anglican diocese of Southern Europe, to welcome the newcomers, to put them at their ease. 'Beautiful evening,' he said, in his too richly cultured voice. (But I loved him for his trousers.) 'Beautiful,' we agreed, and that the place was charming. 'Staying long?' he asked. We looked at one another, then round the crowded hall, then again at one another. I shook my head. 'To-morrow,' I said, 'we have to make a very early start.'

# WORDSWORTH IN THE TROPICS

In the neighbourhood of latitude fifty north, and for the last hundred years or thereabouts, it has been an axiom that Nature is divine and morally uplifting. For good Wordsworthians— and most serious-minded people are now Wordsworthians, either by direct inspiration or at second hand—a walk in the country is the equivalent of going to church, a tour through Westmorland is as good as a pilgrimage to Jerusalem. To commune with the fields and waters, the woodlands and the hills, is to commune, according to our modern and northern ideas, with the visible manifestations of the 'Wisdom and Spirit of the Universe.'

The Wordsworthian who exports this pantheistic worship of Nature to the tropics is liable to have his religious convictions somewhat rudely disturbed. Nature, under a vertical sun, and nourished by the equatorial rains, is not at all like that chaste, mild deity who presides over the *Gemüthlichkeit*, the prettiness, the cosy sublimities of the Lake District. The worst that Wordsworth's goddess ever did to him was to make him hear

> Low breathings coming after me, and sounds
> Of undistinguishable motion, steps
> Almost as silent as the turf they trod ;

was to make him realize, in the shape of 'a huge

peak, black and huge,' the existence of 'unknown modes of being.' He seems to have imagined that this was the worst Nature *could* do. A few weeks in Malaya or Borneo would have undeceived him. Wandering in the hothouse darkness of the jungle, he would not have felt so serenely certain of those ' Presences of Nature,' those ' Souls of Lonely Places,' which he was in the habit of worshipping on the shores of Windermere and Rydal. The sparse inhabitants of the equatorial forest are all believers in devils. When one has visited, in even the most superficial manner, the places where they live, it is difficult not to share their faith. The jungle is marvellous, fantastic, beautiful ; but it is also terrifying, it is also profoundly sinister. There is something in what, for lack of a better word, we must call the character of great forests—even in those of temperate lands—which is foreign, appalling, fundamentally and utterly inimical to intruding man. The life of those vast masses of swarming vegetation is alien to the human spirit and hostile to it. Meredith, in his ' Woods of Westermaine,' has tried reassuringly to persuade us that our terrors are unnecessary, that the hostility of these vegetable forces is more apparent than real, and that if we will but trust Nature we shall find our fears transformed into serenity, joy, and rapture. This may be sound philosophy in the neighbourhood of Dorking ; but it begins to be dubious even in the forests of Germany

—there is too much of them for a human being to feel himself at ease within their enormous glooms ; and when the woods of Borneo are substituted for those of Westermaine, Meredith's comforting doctrine becomes frankly ridiculous.

It is not the sense of solitude that distresses the wanderer in equatorial jungles. Loneliness is bearable enough—for a time, at any rate. There is something actually rather stimulating and exciting about being in an empty place where there is no life but one's own. Taken in reasonably small doses, the Sahara exhilarates, like alcohol. Too much of it, however (I speak, at any rate, for myself), has the depressing effect of the second bottle of Burgundy. But in any case it is not loneliness that oppresses the equatorial traveller : it is too much company ; it is the uneasy feeling that he is an alien in the midst of an innumerable throng of hostile beings. To us who live beneath a temperate sky and in the age of Henry Ford, the worship of Nature comes almost naturally. It is easy to love a feeble and already conquered enemy. But an enemy with whom one is still at war, an unconquered, unconquerable, ceaselessly active enemy—no ; one does not, one should not, love him. One respects him, perhaps ; one has a salutary fear of him ; and one goes on fighting. In our latitudes the hosts of Nature have mostly been vanquished and enslaved. Some few detachments, it is true, still hold the field against us. There are wild woods and mountains, marshes and heaths, even in England. But they are there only on sufferance, because we have chosen, out of our good pleasure, to leave them their freedom. It has not been worth our while to reduce them to slavery. We love them because we are the masters, because we know that at any moment we can overcome them as we overcame their fellows. The inhabitants of the tropics have no such comforting reasons for adoring the sinister forces which hem them in on every side. For us, the notion ' river ' implies (how obviously !) the notion ' bridge.' When we think of a plain, we think of agriculture, towns, and good roads. The corollary of mountain is tunnel ; of swamp, an embankment ; of distance, a railway. At latitude zero, however, the obvious is not the same as with us. Rivers imply wading, swimming, alligators. Plains mean swamps, forests, fevers. Mountains are either dangerous or impassable. To travel is to hack one's way laboriously through a tangled, prickly, and venomous darkness. ' God made the country,' said Cowper, in his rather too blank verse. In New Guinea he would have had his doubts ; he would have longed for the man-made town.

The Wordsworthian adoration of Nature has two principal defects. The first, as we have seen, is that it is only possible in a country where Nature has been nearly or quite enslaved to man. The second is that it is only possible for those

who are prepared to falsify their immediate intuitions of Nature. For Nature, even in the
temperate zone, is always alien and inhuman,
and occasionally diabolic. Meredith explicitly
invites us to explain any unpleasant experiences
away. We are to interpret them, Pangloss
fashion, in terms of a preconceived philosophy ;
after which, all will surely be for the best in the
best of all possible Westermaines. Less openly,
Wordsworth asks us to make the same falsification
of immediate experience. It is only very occasionally that he admits the existence in the world
around him of those ' unknown modes of being '
of which our immediate intuitions of things
make us so disquietingly aware. Normally what
he does is to pump the dangerous Unknown out
of Nature and refill the emptied forms of hills
and woods, flowers and waters, with something
more reassuringly familiar—with humanity, with
Anglicanism. He will not admit that a yellow
primrose is simply a yellow primrose—beautiful,
but essentially strange, having its own alien life
apart. He wants it to possess some sort of soul,
to exist humanly, not simply flowerily. He wants
the earth to be more than earthy, to be a divine
person. But the life of vegetation is radically
unlike the life of man : the earth has a mode of
being that is certainly not the mode of being of
a person. ' Let Nature be your teacher,' says
Wordsworth. The advice is excellent. But how
strangely he himself puts it into practice ! In-

stead of listening humbly to what the teacher says, he shuts his ears and himself dictates the lesson he desires to hear. The pupil knows better than his master ; the worshipper substitutes his own oracles for those of the god. Instead of accepting the lesson as it is given to his immediate intuitions, he distorts it rationalistically into the likeness of a parson's sermon or a professorial lecture. Our direct intuitions of Nature tell us that the world is bottomlessly strange : alien, even when it is kind and beautiful ; having innumerable modes of being that are not our modes ; always mysteriously not personal, not conscious, not moral ; often hostile and sinister ; sometimes even unimaginably, because inhumanly, evil. In his youth, it would seem, Wordsworth left his direct intuitions of the world unwarped.

> The sounding cataract
> Haunted me like a passion : the tall rock,
> The mountain, and the deep and gloomy wood,
> Their colours and their forms, were then to me
> An appetite ; a feeling and a love,
> That had no need of a remoter charm,
> By thought supplied, nor any interest
> Unborrowed from the eye.

As the years passed, however, he began to interpret them in terms of a preconceived philosophy. Procrustes-like, he tortured his feelings and perceptions until they fitted his system. By the time he was thirty,

> The immeasurable height
> Of woods decaying, never to be decayed,
> The stationary blasts of waterfalls—
> The torrents shooting from the clear blue sky,
> The rocks that muttered close upon our ears,
> Black drizzling crags that spake by the wayside
> As if a voice were in them, the sick sight
> And giddy prospect of the raving stream,
> The unfettered clouds and regions of the heavens,
> Tumult and peace, the darkness and the light—
> Were all like workings of one mind, the features
> Of the same face, blossoms upon one tree,
> Characters of the great Apocalypse,
> The types and symbols of eternity,
> Of first, and last, and midst, and without end.

'Something far more deeply interfused' had made its appearance on the Wordsworthian scene. The god of Anglicanism had crept under the skin of things, and all the stimulatingly inhuman strangeness of Nature had become as flatly familiar as a page from a textbook of metaphysics or theology. As familiar and as safely simple. Pantheistically interpreted, our intuitions of Nature's endless varieties of impersonal mysteriousness lose all their exciting and disturbing quality. It makes the world seem delightfully cosy, if you can pretend that all the many alien things about you are really only manifestations of one person. It is fear of the labyrinthine flux and complexity of phenomena that has driven men to philosophy, to science, to theology—fear of the complex reality driving them to invent a simpler, more manageable, and, therefore, consoling fiction. For simple, in comparison with the external reality of which we have direct intuitions, childishly simple is even the most elaborate and subtle system devised by the human mind. Most of the philosophical systems hitherto popular have not been subtle and elaborate even by human standards. Even by human standards they have been crude, bald, preposterously straightforward. Hence their popularity. Their simplicity has rendered them instantly comprehensible. Weary with much wandering in the maze of phenomena, frightened by the inhospitable strangeness of the world, men have rushed into the systems prepared for them by philosophers and founders of religions, as they would rush from a dark jungle into the haven of a well-lit, commodious house. With a sigh of relief and a thankful feeling that here at last is their true home, they settle down in their snug metaphysical villa and go to sleep. And how furious they are when any one comes rudely knocking at the door to tell them that their villa is jerry-built, dilapidated, unfit for human habitation, even non-existent ! Men have been burnt at the stake for even venturing to criticize the colour of the front door or the shape of the third-floor windows.

That man must build himself some sort of metaphysical shelter in the midst of the jungle of immediately apprehended reality is obvious. No

practical activity, no scientific research, no specu-
lation is possible without some preliminary
hypothesis about the nature and the purpose of
things. The human mind cannot deal with the
universe directly, nor even with its own immediate intuitions of the universe. Whenever it is a
question of thinking about the world or of practically modifying it, men can only work on a sym-
bolic plan of the universe, only on a simplified,
two-dimensional map of things abstracted by
the mind out of the complex and multifarious
reality of immediate intuition. History shows
that these hypotheses about the nature of things
are valuable even when, as later experience
reveals, they are false. Man approaches the
unattainable truth through a succession of errors.
Confronted by the strange complexity of things,
he invents, quite arbitrarily, a simple hypothesis
to explain and justify the world. Having invented, he proceeds to act and think in terms of
this hypothesis, as though it were correct. Experience gradually shows him where his hypothesis is unsatisfactory and how it should be
modified. Thus, great scientific discoveries have
been made by men seeking to verify quite erroneous theories about the nature of things. The
discoveries have necessitated a modification of
the original hypotheses, and further discoveries
have been made in the effort to verify the modifications—discoveries which, in their turn, have
led to yet further modifications. And so on,

indefinitely. Philosophical and religious hypotheses, being less susceptible of experimental verification than the hypotheses of science, have undergone far less modification. For example, the pantheistic hypothesis of Wordsworth is an ancient doctrine, which human experience has hardly modified throughout history. And rightly, no doubt. For it is obvious that there must be some sort of unity underlying the diversity of phenomena ; for if there were not, the world would be quite unknowable. Indeed, it is precisely in the knowableness of things, in the very fact that they are known, that their fundamental unity consists. The world which we know, and which our minds have fabricated out of goodness knows what mysterious things in themselves, possesses the unity which our minds have imposed upon it. It is part of our thought, hence fundamentally homogeneous. Yes, the world is obviously one. But at the same time it is no less obviously diverse. For if the world were absolutely one, it would no longer be knowable, it would cease to exist. Thought must be divided against itself before it can come to any knowledge of itself. Absolute oneness is absolute nothingness : homogeneous perfection, as the Hindus perceived and courageously recognized, is equivalent to non-existence, is nirvana. The Christian idea of a perfect heaven that is something other than a non-existence is a contradiction in terms. The world in which we live may be fundamentally one, but it is a unity divided up into a great many diverse fragments. A tree, a table, a newspaper, a piece of artificial silk are all made of wood. But they are, none the less, distinct and separate objects. It is the same with the world at large. Our immediate intuitions are of diversity. We have only to open our eyes to recognize a multitude of different phenomena. These intuitions of diversity are as correct, as well justified, as is our intellectual conviction of the fundamental homogeneity of the various parts of the world with one another and with ourselves. Circumstances have led humanity to set an ever-increasing premium on the conscious and intellectual comprehension of things. Modern man's besetting temptation is to sacrifice his direct perceptions and spontaneous feelings to his reasoned reflections ; to prefer in all circumstances the verdict of his intellect to that of his immediate intuitions. ' L'homme est visiblement fait pour penser,' says Pascal ; ' c'est toute sa dignité et tout son mérite ; et tout son devoir est de penser comme il faut.' Noble words ; but do they happen to be true ? Pascal seems to forget that man has something else to do besides think : he must live. Living may not be so dignified or so meritorious as thinking (particularly when you happen to be, like Pascal, a chronic invalid) ; but it is, perhaps unfortunately, a necessary process. If one would live well, one must live completely, with the whole being—

with the body and the instincts, as well as with
the conscious mind. A life lived, as far as may
be, exclusively from the consciousness and in
accordance with the considered judgments of
the intellect, is a stunted life, a half-dead life.
This is a fact that can be confirmed by daily
observation. But consciousness, the intellect,
the spirit, have acquired an inordinate prestige ;
and such is men's snobbish respect for authority,
such is their pedantic desire to be consistent, that
they go on doing their best to lead the exclusively
conscious, spiritual, and intellectual life, in spite
of its manifest disadvantages. To know is
pleasant ; it is exciting to be conscious ; the
intellect is a valuable instrument, and for certain
purposes the hypotheses which it fabricates are
of great practical value. Quite true. But,
therefore, say the moralists and men of science,
drawing conclusions only justified by their desire
for consistency, therefore *all* life should be lived
from the head, consciously, *all* phenomena should
at *all* times be interpreted in terms of the intellect's hypotheses. The religious teachers are of
a slightly different opinion. All life, according
to them, should be lived spiritually, not intellectually. Why ? On the grounds, as we discover when we push our analysis far enough,
that certain occasional psychological states, currently called spiritual, are extremely agreeable
and have valuable consequences in the realm
of social behaviour. The unprejudiced observer

finds it hard to understand why these people should set such store by consistency of thought and action. Because oysters are occasionally pleasant, it does not follow that one should make of oysters one's exclusive diet. Nor should one take castor-oil every day because castor-oil is occasionally good for one. Too much consistency is as bad for the mind as it is for the body. Consistency is contrary to nature, contrary to life. The only completely consistent people are the dead. Consistent intellectualism and spirituality may be socially valuable, up to a point ; but they make, gradually, for individual death. And individual death, when the slow murder has been consummated, is finally social death. So that the social utility of pure intellectualism and pure spirituality is only apparent and temporary. What is needed is, as ever, a compromise. Life must be lived in different ways at different moments. The only satisfactory way of existing in the modern, highly specialized world is to live with two personalities. A Dr. Jekyll that does the metaphysical and scientific thinking, that transacts business in the city, adds up figures, designs machines, and so forth. And a natural, spontaneous Mr. Hyde to do the physical, instinctive living in the intervals of work. The two personalities should lead their unconnected lives apart, without poaching on one another's preserves or inquiring too closely into one another's activities. Only by living discretely and inconsistently can we preserve both the man and the citizen, both the intellectual and the spontaneous animal being, alive within us. The solution may not be very satisfactory ; but it is, I believe now (though once I thought differently), the best that, in the modern circumstances, can be devised.

The poet's place, it seems to me, is with the Mr. Hydes of human nature. He should be, as Blake remarked of Milton, ' of the devil's party without knowing it '—or preferably with the full consciousness of being of the devil's party. There are so many intellectual and moral angels battling for rationalism, good citizenship, and pure spirituality ; so many and such eminent ones, so very vocal and authoritative ! The poor devil in man needs all the support and advocacy he can get. The artist is his natural champion. When an artist deserts to the side of the angels, it is the most odious of treasons. How unforgivable, for example, is Tolstoy ! Tolstoy, the perfect Mr. Hyde, the complete embodiment, if ever there was one, of non-intellectual, non-moral, instinctive life—Tolstoy, who betrayed his own nature, betrayed his art, betrayed life itself, in order to fight against the devil's party of his earlier allegiances, under the standard of Dr. Jesus-Jekyll. Wordsworth's betrayal was not so spectacular : he was never so wholly of the devil's party as Tolstoy. Still, it was bad enough. It is difficult to forgive him for so

utterly repenting his youthful passions and en-
thusiasms, and becoming, personally as well as
politically, the anglican tory. One remembers
B. R. Haydon's account of the poet's reactions
to that charming classical sculpture of Cupid
and Psyche. 'The devils!' he said malignantly, after a long-drawn contemplation of
their marble embrace. 'The devils!' And he
was not using the word in the complimentary
sense in which I have employed it here : he was
expressing his hatred of passion and life, he was
damning the young man he had himself been—
the young man who had hailed the French
Revolution with delight and begotten an illegiti-
mate child. From being an ardent lover of the
nymphs, he had become one of those all too
numerous

> woodmen who expel
> Love's gentle dryads from the haunts of life,
> And vex the nightingales in every dell.

Yes, even the nightingales he vexed. Even the
nightingales, though the poor birds can never,
like those all too human dryads, have led him
into sexual temptation. Even the innocuous
nightingales were moralized, spiritualized, turned
into citizens and anglicans—and along with the
nightingales, the whole of animate and inanimate
Nature.

The change in Wordsworth's attitude towards
Nature is symptomatic of his general apostasy.
Beginning as what I may call a natural aesthete,

he transformed himself, in the course of years, into a moralist, a thinker. He used his intellect to distort his exquisitely acute and subtle intuitions of the world, to explain away their often disquieting strangeness, to simplify them into a comfortable metaphysical unreality. Nature had endowed him with the poet's gift of seeing more than ordinarily far into the brick walls of external reality, of intuitively comprehending the character of the bricks, of feeling the quality of their being, and establishing the appropriate relationship with them. But he preferred to think his gifts away. He preferred, in the interests of a preconceived religious theory, to ignore the disquieting strangeness of things, to interpret the impersonal diversity of Nature in terms of a divine, anglican unity. He chose, in a word, to be a philosopher, comfortably at home with a man-made and, therefore, thoroughly comprehensible system, rather than a poet adventuring for adventure's sake through the mysterious world revealed by his direct and undistorted intuitions.

It is a pity that he never travelled beyond the boundaries of Europe. A voyage through the tropics would have cured him of his too easy and comfortable pantheism. A few months in the jungle would have convinced him that the diversity and utter strangeness of Nature are at least as real and significant as its intellectually discovered unity. Nor would he have felt so

certain, in the damp and stifling darkness, among
the leeches and the malevolently tangled rattans,
of the divinely anglican character of that fundamental unity. He would have learned once more
to treat Nature naturally, as he treated it in his
youth ; to react to it spontaneously, loving
where love was the appropriate emotion, fear-
ing, hating, fighting whenever Nature presented
itself to his intuition as being, not merely strange,
but hostile, inhumanly evil. A voyage would
have taught him this. But Wordsworth never
left his native continent. Europe is so well
gardened that it resembles a work of art, a
scientific theory, a neat metaphysical system.
Man has re-created Europe in his own image.
Its tamed and temperate Nature confirmed
Wordsworth in his philosophizings. The poet,
the devil's partisan were doomed ; the angels
triumphed. Alas !

Human nature does not change, or, at any rate, history is too short for any changes to be perceptible. The earliest known specimens of art and literature are still comprehensible. The fact that we can understand them all and can recognize in some of them an unsurpassed artistic excellence is proof enough that not only men's feelings and instincts, but also their intellectual and imaginative powers, were in the remotest times precisely what they are now. In the fine arts it is only the convention, the form, the incidentals that change : the fundamentals of passion, of intellect and imagination remain unaltered.

It is the same with the arts of life as with the fine arts. Conventions and traditions, prejudices and ideals and religious beliefs, moral systems and codes of good manners, varying according to the geographical and historical circumstances, mould into different forms the unchanging material of human instinct, passion, and desire. It is a stiff, intractable material— Egyptian granite, rather than Hindu bronze. The artists who carved the colossal statues of Rameses II. may have wished to represent the Pharaoh standing on one leg and waving two or three pairs of arms over his head, as the Indians still represent the dancing Krishna. But with the best will in the world they could not have imposed such a form upon the granite. Similarly, those artists in social life whom we call statesmen, moralists, founders of religions, have often wished to mould human nature into forms of superhuman elegance ; but the material has proved too stubborn for them, and they have had to be content with only a relatively small alteration in the form which their predecessors had given it. At any given historical moment human behaviour is a compromise (enforced from without by law and custom, from within by belief in religious or philosophical myths) between the raw instinct on the one hand and the unattainable ideal on the other—a compromise, in our sculptural metaphor, between the unshaped block of stone and the many-armed dancing Krishna.

Like all the other great human activities, love is the product of unchanging passions, instincts, and desires (unchanging, that is to say, in the mass of humanity ; for, of course, they vary greatly in quantity and quality from individual to individual), and of laws and conventions, beliefs and ideals, which the circumstances of time and place, or the arbitrary fiats of great personalities, have imposed on a more or less willing society. The history of love, if it were ever written (and doubtless some learned German, unread, alas, by me, *has* written it, and in several volumes), would be like the current histories of art—a record of succeeding 'styles' and 'schools,' of 'influences,' 'revolutions,' 'technical discoveries.' Love's psychological and physiological material remains the same ; but every epoch treats it in a different manner, just as every epoch cuts its unvarying cloth and silk and linen into garments of the most diverse fashion. By way of illustration, I may mention that vogue of homosexuality which seems, from all accounts, to have been universal in the Hellenic world. Plutarch attributes the inception of this mode to the custom (novel in the fifth century, according to Thucydides) of exercising naked in the palestra.[1] But whatever may have been its origin, there can be no doubt that this particular fashion in love spread widely among people who were not in the least congenitally disposed to homosexuality. Convention and public opinion moulded the material of love into forms which a later age has chosen to call 'unnatural.' A recrudescence of this amorous mode was very noticeable in Europe during the years immediately following the War. Among the determining causes of this recrudescence a future Plutarch will undoubtedly number the writings of Proust and André Gide.

[1] Plutarch, who wrote some five hundred years after the event, is by no means an unquestionable authority. The habit of which he and Thucydides speak may have facilitated the spread of the homosexual fashion. But that the fashion existed before the fifth century is made sufficiently clear by Homer, not to mention Sappho. Like many modern oriental peoples, the ancient Greeks were evidently, in Sir Richard Burton's expressive phrase, 'omnifutuent.'

The present fashions in love are not so definite and universal as those in clothes. It is as though our age were dubiously hesitating between crinolines and hobble skirts, trunk hose and Oxford trousers. Two distinct and hostile conceptions of love coexist in the minds of men and women, two sets of ideals, of conventions, of public opinions, struggle for the right to mould the psychological and physiological material of love. One is the conception evolved by the nineteenth century out of the ideals of Christianity on the one hand and romanticism on the other. The other is that still rather inchoate and negative conception which contemporary youth is in process of forming out of the materials provided by modern psychology. The public opinion, the conventions, ideals, and prejudices which gave active force to the first convention and enabled it, to some extent at least, to modify the actual practice of love, had already lost much of their strength when they were rudely shattered, at any rate in the minds of the young, by the shock of the War. As usually happens, practice preceded theory, and the new conception of love was called in to justify existing post-War manners. Having gained a footing, the new conception is now a cause of new behaviour among the youngest adolescent generation, instead of being, as it was for the generation of the War, an explanation of war-time behaviour made after the fact.

Let us try to analyse these two coexisting and

conflicting conceptions of love. The older conception was, as I have said, the product of Christianity and romanticism—a curious mixture of contradictions, of the ascetic dread of passion and the romantic worship of passion. Its ideal was a strict monogamy, such as St. Paul grudgingly conceded to amorous humanity, sanctified and made eternal by one of those terrific exclusive passions which are the favourite theme of poetry and drama. It is an ideal which finds its most characteristic expression in the poetry of that infinitely respectable rebel, that profoundly anglican worshipper of passion, Robert Browning. It was Rousseau who first started the cult of passion for passion's sake. Before his time the great passions, such as that of Paris for Helen, of Dido for Æneas, of Paolo and Francesca for one another, had been regarded rather as disastrous maladies than as enviable states of soul. Rousseau, followed by all the romantic poets of France and England, transformed the grand passion from what it had been in the Middle Ages — a demoniac possession — into a divine ecstasy, and promoted it from the rank of a disease to that of the only true and natural form of love. The nineteenth-century conception of love was thus doubly mystical, with the mysticism of Christian asceticism and sacramentalism, and with the romantic mysticism of Nature. It claimed an absolute rightness on the grounds of its divinity and of its naturalness.

Now, if there is one thing that the study of history and psychology makes abundantly clear, it is that there are no such things as either 'divine' or 'natural' forms of love. Innumerable gods have sanctioned and forbidden innumerable kinds of sexual behaviour, and innumerable philosophers and poets have advocated the return to the most diverse kinds of 'nature.' Every form of amorous behaviour, from chastity and monogamy to promiscuity and the most fantastic 'perversions,' is found both among animals and men. In any given human society, at any given moment, love, as we have seen, is the result of the interaction of the unchanging instinctive and physiological material of sex with the local conventions of morality and religion, the local laws, prejudices, and ideals. The degree of permanence of these conventions, religious myths, and ideals is proportional to their social utility in the given circumstances of time and place.

The new twentieth-century conception of love is realistic. It recognizes the diversity of love, not merely in the social mass from age to age, but from individual to contemporary individual, according to the dosage of the different instincts with which each is born, and the upbringing he has received. The new generation knows that there is no such thing as Love with a large L, and that what the Christian romantics of the last century regarded as the uniquely natural form of love is, in fact, only one of the indefinite number of possible amorous fashions, produced by specific circumstances at that particular time. Psycho-analysis has taught it that all the forms of sexual behaviour previously regarded as wicked, perverse, unnatural, are statistically normal (and normality is solely a question of statistics), and that what is commonly called amorous normality is far from being a spontaneous, instinctive form of behaviour, but must be acquired by a process of education. Having contracted the habit of talking freely and more or less scientifically about sexual matters, the young no longer regard love with that feeling of rather guilty excitement and thrilling shame which was for an earlier generation the normal reaction to the subject. Moreover, the practice of birth-control has robbed amorous indulgence of most of the sinfulness traditionally supposed to be inherent in it by robbing it of its socially disastrous effects. The tree shall be known by its fruits : where there are no fruits, there is obviously no tree. Love has ceased to be the rather fearful, mysterious thing it was, and become a perfectly normal, almost commonplace, activity—an activity, for many young people, especially in America, of the same nature as dancing or tennis, a sport, a recreation, a pastime. For those who hold this conception of love, liberty and toleration are prime necessities. A strenuous offensive against the old taboos and repressions is everywhere in progress.

Such, then, are the two conceptions of love which oppose one another to-day. Which is the better ? Without presuming to pass judgment, I will content myself with pointing out the defects of each. The older conception was bad, in so far as it inflicted unnecessary and undeserved sufferings on the many human beings whose congenital and acquired modes of love-making did not conform to the fashionable Christian-romantic pattern which was regarded as being uniquely entitled to call itself Love. The new conception is bad, it seems to me, in so far as it takes love too easily and lightly. On love regarded as an amusement the last word is surely this of Robert Burns :

> I waive the quantum of the sin,
>     The hazard of concealing ;
> But oh ! it hardens all within
>     And petrifies the feeling.

Nothing is more dreadful than a cold, unimpassioned indulgence. And love infallibly becomes cold and unimpassioned when it is too lightly made. It is not good, as Pascal remarked, to have too much liberty. Love is the product of two opposed forces—of an instinctive impulsion and a social resistance acting on the individual by means of ethical imperatives justified by philosophical or religious myths. When, with the destruction of the myths, resistance is removed, the impulse wastes itself on emptiness ; and love which is only the product of conflicting forces, is not born. The twentieth century is reproducing in a new form the error of the early nineteenth-century romantics. Following Rousseau, the romantics imagined that exclusive passion was the 'natural' mode of love, just as virtue and reasonableness were the 'natural' forms of men's social behaviour. Get rid of priests and kings, and men will be for ever good and happy ; poor Shelley's faith in this palpable nonsense remained unshaken to the end. He believed also in the complementary paralogism that you had only to get rid of social restraints and erroneous mythology to make the Grand Passion universally chronic. Like the Mussets and Sands, he failed to see that the Grand Passion was produced by the restraints that opposed themselves to the sexual impulse, just as the deep lake is produced by the dam that bars the passage of the stream, and the flight of the aeroplane by the air which resists the impulsion given to it by the motor. There would be no air-resistance in a vacuum ; but precisely for that reason the machine would not leave the ground, or even move at all. Where there are no psychological or external restraints, the Grand Passion does not come into existence and must be artificially cultivated, as George Sands and Musset cultivated it—with what painful and grotesque results the episode of Venice made only too ludicrously manifest.

'J'aime et je veux pâlir ; j'aime et je veux souffrir,' says Musset, with his usual hysterically masochistic emphasis. Our young contemporaries do not wish to suffer or grow pale ; on the contrary, they have a most determined desire to grow pink and enjoy themselves. But too much enjoyment 'blunts the fine point of seldom pleasure.' Unrestrained indulgence kills not merely passion, but, in the end, even amusement. Too much liberty is as life-destroying as too much restraint. The present fashion in love-making is likely to be short, because love that is psychologically too easy is not interesting. Such, at any rate, was evidently the opinion of the French, who, bored by the sexual licence produced by the Napoleonic upheavals, reverted (so far, at any rate, as the upper and middle classes were concerned) to an almost anglican strictness under Louis-Philippe. We may anticipate an analogous reaction in the not distant future. What new or what revived mythology will serve to create those internal restraints without which sexual impulse cannot be transformed into love ? Christian morality and ascetic ideals will doubtless continue to play their part, but there will no less certainly be other moralities and ideals. For example, Mr. D. H. Lawrence's new mythology of nature (new in its expression, but reassuringly old in substance) is a doctrine that seems to me fruitful in possibilities. The 'natural love' which he sets up as a norm is a passion less self-conscious and high-falutin, less obviously and precariously artificial, than that 'natural love' of the romantics, in which Platonic and Christian notions were essential ingredients. The restraints which Mr. Lawrence would impose on sexual impulse, so as to transform it into love, are not the restraints of religious spirituality. They are restraints of a more fundamental, less artificial nature—emotional, not intellectual. The impulse is to be restrained from promiscuous manifestations because, if it were not, promiscuity would 'harden all within and petrify the feeling.' The restraint is of the same personal nature as the impulse. The conflict is between a part of the personality and the personality as an organized whole. It does not pretend, as the romantic and Christian conflict pretends, to be a battle between a diabolical Lower Self and certain transcendental Absolutes, of which the only thing that philosophy can tell us is that they are absolutely unknowable, and therefore, for our purposes, non-existent. It only claims to be, what in fact it is, a psychological conflict taking place in the more or less known and finite world of human interests. This doctrine has several great advantages over previous systems of inward restraint. It does not postulate the existence of any transcendental, non-human entity. This is a merit which will be increasingly appreciated as the significance of Kant's and Nietzsche's destructive criticism is more widely realized.

People will cease to be interested in unknowable absolutes ; but they will never lose interest in their own personalities. True, that ' personality as a whole,' in whose interests the sexual impulse is to be restrained and turned into love, is, strictly speaking, a mythological figure. Consisting, as we do, of a vast colony of souls—souls of individual cells, of organs, of groups of organs, hunger-souls, sex-souls, power-souls, herd-souls, of whose multifarious activities our consciousness (the Soul with a large S) is only very imperfectly and indirectly aware—we are not in a position to know the real nature of our personality as a whole. The only thing we can do is to hazard a hypothesis, to create a mythological figure, call it Human Personality, and hope that circumstances will not, by destroying us, prove our imaginative guesswork too hopelessly wrong. But myth for myth, Human Personality is preferable to God. We do at least know something of Human Personality, whereas of God we know nothing and, knowing nothing, are at liberty to invent as freely as we like. If men had always tried to deal with the problem of love in terms of known human rather than of grotesquely imagined divine interests, there would have been less ' making of eunuchs for the kingdom of heaven's sake,' less persecution of ' sinners,' less burning and imprisoning of the heretics of ' unnatural ' love, less Grundyism, less Comstockery, and, at the same time, less dirty Don-Juanism, less of that curiously malignant and vengeful love-making so characteristic of the debauchee under a Christian dispensation. Reacting against the absurdities of the old mythology, the young have run into absurdities no less inordinate at the other end of the scale. A sordid and ignoble realism offers no resistance to the sexual impulse, which now spends itself purposelessly, without producing love, or even, in the long-run, amusement, without enhancing vitality or quickening and deepening the rhythms of living. Only a new mythology of nature, such as, in modern times, Blake, Robert Burns, and Lawrence have defined it, an untranscendental and (relatively speaking) realistic mythology of Energy, Life, and Human Personality, will provide, it seems to me, the inward resistances necessary to turn sexual impulse into love, and provide them in a form which the critical intelligence of Post-Nietzschean youth can respect. By means of such a conception a new fashion in love may be created, a mode more beautiful and convenient, more healthful and elegant, than any seen among men since the days of remote and pagan antiquity.

# FRANCIS AND GRIGORY, OR
## THE TWO HUMILITIES

St. Francis we call him. But the little poor man of Assisi, the littlest of the littler brothers —that was what he liked to call himself. Humbly. He believed in being humble. He was proud of his humility.

Now, humility is an excellent thing, so long as it's the right sort of humility. And so is the right sort of pride. But what are the right sorts of humility and pride? They are the sorts, it is evident, of which *I* approve. But are they anything else? I do not know, but I hope so. In the following pages I have set down the reasons for my hopes. Meanwhile, let me say at once that I don't like either the humbleness of the little poor man, or his pride. If I were in the habit of using clerical phraseology, I should say that they were not 'true' pride, 'true' humility. For True Pride, my brethren, is surely unmixed with vanity. I dislike vain people as much as I like those who are proud of their humanity and know how to stick up for their human rights and dignity. Was Francis's pride of the true variety? '*Cum esset gloriosus animo,*' in the words of a contemporary, '*et nollet aliquem se praecellere,*' I doubt it. All his history testifies to his vanity. His youthful dissipations, for example—what drove him into those? Pure snobbery. To be debauched was a sign then, as in later times, of nobility. Vain, the son of a shopkeeper, he was ambitious to outspend, outdrink, outroar, and outfornicate the choicest imps of the Umbrian nobility. And when he was a prisoner of war at Perugia, in 1202, 'You'll see,' he was wont to say to his companions, 'one day I shall be worshipped by the whole world.' Later, he found in dreams of knight-errantry imaginary compensations for the middle-class reality of his existence. An opportunity to realize these dreams in actual life presented itself; Francis seized it. He ordered at great expense a sumptuous knight-errant's trousseau. His appearance in it was dazzling. 'I know,' he said prophetically, 'that I shall become a great prince.' And with that he rode out of Assisi to join the expedition of Walter de Brienne in Apulia. He rode twenty miles, as far as Spoleto, and then, after one day's knight-errantry, returned to the paternal roof. Sabatier suggests that he was 'ragged' by his noble companions. It is very possible. For some time after the ill-fated expedition he seems, at any rate, to have lived in a state of pained retrospective shame and brooding humiliation. But little by little the old passion reasserted itself. To be 'a great prince,' to be 'worshipped by the whole world,' to allow nobody to excel him. But how should he realize these longings? He had tried the knightly way and failed, ignominiously. In his misery he turned to religion, and there, in religion, discovered a new field for achieving the personal distinction for which his soul so ardently and incessantly longed. The world refused to recognize him as Assisi's greatest soldier. Very well. It should recognize him as Assisi's greatest man of God.

Between the modern professional sportsman and a certain type of Christian ascetic there is an extraordinary resemblance. The Lausiac History reads like a record of post-war athletics. Eremitic life in the Thebaid was an affair of record-making and record-breaking. Brother A only washes on Easter Mondays. Very well; Brother B will not wash at all. Brother C lives on one ounce of bread per diem and fasts three days a week. The emulous Brother D goes into training and ends by being able to fast four days a week, and to live on an even smaller ration for the remaining three. Brother X sets up a world's record by drinking only as much water as condenses each night in the form of dew on a small sponge. And so on. We might be in the world whose activities are recorded on the sporting pages of evening papers.

It is worthy of remark that modern record-breakers have been ready to undergo almost greater hardships for the sake of money or, more often, of mere newspaper celebrity than the monks of the Thebaid underwent for the sake —nominally, at any rate—of their religious principles. Contemporary professional fasters have beaten the ascetics hollow. And is there anything in Palladius to compare with the achievement of those American dancing-couples, who keep up their non-stop fox-trotting for days at a stretch ?

St. Francis was something of a record-breaker. He was happy in that private consciousness of having done something uniquely arduous, which is the Alpine climber's reward for all his labours. When he had kissed the leper, he felt like the first man up the Aiguille Mummery. But the approval of his own conscience was not enough ; Francis could never forget his desire to be ' a great prince,' to be acclaimed by all the world. He revelled in the publicity which his almsgiving and afterwards his church-repairing, his theatrical renunciation of his patrimony, his begging and his ascetic practices brought him. He had not been able to make a success of knight-errantry ; but to suffer voluntarily was within his powers. He could achieve celebrity and break records in asceticism and self-abasement, and in nothing else. Hence his admiration for self-abasement and asceticism. Perfection, he told Brother Leo, is not in miracles, not in science, not in converting the heathen (he had achieved no success in any of these departments), but in being shut out by the porter in the wet and cold of a winter night, in suffering voluntarily. Particularly, he might have added, in public. His disciples were instructed to call him names and reproach him with his sins in the presence of the congregation.

The record-breaking was to have a numerous audience. There are some people whose ruling passion is publicity. They will go to any lengths in order to be talked of. It is not uncommon to read in the American papers of adolescents who have committed burglaries, hold-ups, and even murders for the sake of ' getting into the news.' The motives which drive these youths to crime drove Francis to sanctity. Luckily for himself and perhaps also for the Western world, he had a fundamentally virtuous temperament. But a virtuous temperament is a negative thing. Francis would never have fulfilled his yearnings for celebrity, would never have been canonized or even heard of, if he had been merely virtuous. He was also a man of power ; there was a daemon in him, and he spoke as one having authority. To those who speak in that way men listen. ' Such was the devotion in which he was held,' writes Thomas of Spoleto, describing the Saint's visit to Bologna in 1220, ' that men and women followed him in crowds, and any one who succeeded in touching the hem of his garment esteemed himself happy.' Happy, too, must the man have esteemed himself whose youthful ambition it was to be ' worshipped by the whole world.' Success enhanced, if not the actual power that was in him, at any rate his sense of it.

This is how the littlest of the littler brothers addressed the future Gregory IX. when, at the

Chapter of 1218, that statesmanlike cleric suggested that Francis would do well to give more weight to the learned members of the community, and should model his policy on that of the older monastic orders. 'The Lord has called me by the way of simplicity and humility. In them He has shown me the truth for me and for those who would believe and imitate me. So do not speak to me of the rule of St. Benedict, of St. Augustine, of St. Bernard, or any other, but only of that which God in His mercy has seen fit to reveal to me, and of which He has told me that He meant, in it, to make a new pact with the world, and He does not wish that we should have any other. But through your learning and wisdom God will confound you. For the rest, I am confident that God will chastise you.' Such is Francis's 'way of humility'! One likes him when he treads this way. For power, the native power of the individual spirit, is always admirable and beautiful, so long as it is not abused. There were occasions when Francis did abuse his power, when he seems to have employed it for the mere fun of feeling himself powerful and a 'great prince'— as when, for example, he humiliated poor Masseo because he was so handsome and clever, or when, in Cyprus, on their way to Egypt, he compelled Brother Barbaro to eat a gobbet of ass's dung for having spoken ill of a companion. These are instances of mere bullying, not at all worthy of a 'great prince.'

But for the most part Francis used his power more nobly. When he used it 'agin the government,' anarchically, or to bring down the pride, to puncture the fat complacency, of the rich and learned, one can only delight in its manifestations. And how melancholy is the spectacle of poor Francis, at the end of his career, renouncing his power in the name of obedience to authority, betraying his daemon of individual anarchy to the gross and beastly forces of organized society! He tried hard to persuade himself that he did right in giving in to the Church. 'A man gives up all he has, a man loses his life' (Jesus had told his disciples that they must lose their lives if they would gain life) 'when he places himself entirely in the hands of his superior and renders him obedience. And when the inferior sees things that would be better or more useful for his soul than those his superior commands him, let him make the sacrifice of his will to God.' But in his heart he knew that all this, so far as he himself was concerned, was a sophistry and that he had done wrong to betray the daemon in him. A man may eat dung voluntarily—for a bet, to break a record or please his God, for the pleasure of asserting his will in the conquest of instinctive disgust—and not be defiled, not be outraged; may even feel himself strengthened and ennobled by doing so, may eat it with joy. It was with joy that Francis had kissed the leper's rotting hand. But Brother Barbaro had been commanded to eat the ass's dung ; and now, in his turn, at the autumn Chapter of 1220, Francis was being treated as he had treated Barbaro. Reluctantly, against his will, he ate dirt. For him, the man of power, the man with a daemon in him, it was an infamy. So long as it was a matter of obeying his own will, he found humility admirable. So long as he *wanted* to abase himself, he *liked* abasing himself. But to submit to other people's will against his own desires—that was a very different matter.[1]

To abase yourself on principle, because such is your will, to mortify your flesh and thwart your instincts in order to assert your conscious personality—is this humility ? It sounds to me more like the will to power. But the self-abasement, the service ? They are accidental, not essential. If Francis had made a success of his soldiering, his will to power would have expressed itself in the violent domination of others. The assertion of the personal will is as much the essence of the saint's ascetic humility as it is of the Roman's dignity and pride. *Et mihi res, non me rebus, subjungere conor*, is a motto which Francis might have made his own. It is a motto, indeed, which any one might adopt ; for it is an excellent

[1] When Francis resigned his control of the order, what were his feelings ? Sabatier says one thing, Goetz another. I follow Sabatier—partly because I think his version, psychologically, more probable, but chiefly (alas for Historical Truth !) because it makes a better story and fits in more aptly with what I wanted to say !

motto. A man ought to strive to subdue things
to himself—reckoning among 'things' his own
body and his own instincts, and giving to his
conscious will the name of 'self.' He ought—
at any rate for part of the time. But there are
also occasions—and this is what the Franciscan,
no less than the Roman, no less than the Samuel-
Smilesian, morality refuses to admit—when a
man ought to permit himself to be subdued to
things. There are occasions when it is right
that he should sacrifice his will, his conscious
desire to dominate exterior circumstances and
the instinctive and passional forces of his own
being ; there are times when that which is
divine in him, the Life, demands this sacrifice.
The greatest sins, perhaps the only sins, are the
sins against Life. Those who strive consistently
to subdue things to themselves infallibly commit
these sins. For among the 'things' which they
subdue are essential elements of their own
living selves. They sacrifice the whole for that
small part of their being which has intellectually
formulated principles and a conscious will. To
be humble and virtuous in the Franciscan style
a man must deliberately and consistently subdue
things to self. He must never forget to be spiritual,
he must never relax his will ; he must unremittingly eschew all passion and the things of the
flesh. That is to say, he must sacrifice one half
of his being to the other. But is it not possible
to imagine a better because a less murderous

virtue, a humility less suspiciously like the will to power? The saint and the stoic agree in being humble towards 'themselves.' But ought there not to be, at the same time, a compensating humility towards 'things'?

For Francis such a humility would have seemed merely wicked. The Church might feel a little dubious about his doctrine, but not about his morality; he was orthodoxly holy. Good Christians have at all times, inconsistently, practised humility to things; but none but heretics have preached it. The Russian Khlyst, for example.

Grigory Rasputin, the sect's most recent and most remarkable saint, preached 'salvation through sin.' Human beings, he taught, must humble their spiritual pride before the 'lower' elements of their natures, must yield themselves to circumstances and to the impulses, the feelings, which circumstances evoke in them. Those who aspire to be consistently 'good' and 'spiritual,' those whose ambition it is to lead, at all times, and according to fixed principles, the consciously willed 'higher life,' are possessed by a Luciferian pride; for they are striving, in their hybristic insolence, to be more than human. But Christianity enjoins humility. Let the spirit, therefore, abase itself before the flesh, the will before the impulsions of instinct, the intellect before the passions. To abandon oneself to sin is the truest humility. And when one has sinned one must repent. For repentance is pleasing to God, and without repentance is no salvation. But without sin there can be no repentance. Therefore . . . The conclusion is obvious. Desiring salvation, Rasputin practised what he preached, and sinned —most conspicuously, as was the custom of the Khlysty, in relation to the seventh commandment.

At the beginning of his career he seems to have sinned in a not unpleasingly Panic and Arcadian manner. But later, when he had exchanged the country for the town and had become the most influential man in Russia, the primitive candour evaporated and from innocent his sinning became civilizedly sophisticated and, if we can believe the stories told of him, sordid and rather dirty. A great many of these stories are obviously such lies as always crystallize round the name of any extraordinary man after it has remained long enough soaking in the malodorous imagination of the respectable bourgeoisie. But, after making all necessary discounts, there is, I think, good evidence that the Staretz degenerated in proportion as he achieved success. To the pastoral orgies of his youth his later urban misbehaviours stand in much the same relation as an eighteenth-century Black Mass or fashionable Witches' Sabbath to the old pre-Christian fertility cult, of which mediæval witchcraft was the steadily degenerating, the more and more self-consciously wicked, survival.

You may disapprove of Rasputin personally. (And after reading Fülop-Miller's impartial and

tolerably well documented biography, it is difficult to disapprove very violently. The Staretz
turns out to have been, on the whole, a sympathetic character. At any rate, one cannot fail
to like and admire him a million times more
than any of the aristocratic rogues, fools, weak-
lings and neurasthenics, in the midst of whom
he accomplished his extraordinary destiny. At
least Rasputin was a man. A power, moreover. A man with a daemon in his belly. And
daemons are always admirable.) Anyhow, whatever may be your disapproval of Grigory the
man, Grigory the moral philosopher is a personage who must be taken seriously. For he
propounds an alternative to the Christian ethic ;
he preaches a moral heresy which it is difficult,
if one has any sense of psychological realities,
not to prefer, in many respects, to the moral
orthodoxy of Christendom and contemporary
Businessdom.

That the Khlysty were *Christian* heretics is unfortunate. For it meant that all their thinking was
necessarily done in terms of the orthodoxy from
which they differed. Thus, they assumed as an
axiom the absurd Christian dualism of mind and
matter, wicked flesh and good spirit. Their
ritual, which should have been joyously and
spontaneously dionysiac, was liable, in conse-
quence, to degenerate into a self-consciously
naughty misbehaviour. They talked of life and
religion, they lived the one and performed the

ritual actions of the other, in terms of sin and repentance and posthumous salvation. The significance of their teaching is in this way largely obscured. We should, however, try to separate the substance of the doctrine from its unfortunately Christian form. That substance can be expressed in the Latin poet's hexameter, slightly modified for the occasion. *Et mihi res, et me rebus subjungere conor.* I strive to subdue things to myself and also, when occasion demands, myself to things. Such is Grigory's humility.

It is unnecessary for me to enumerate all the advantages of occasionally subjugating the consciously willing self to 'things'—or, in other words, to outside circumstances and the immediate reactions to those circumstances of the instinctive and passional side of the personality. We are born with a nature composed of certain elements. If we refuse to admit the right of some of these elements to exist, if we try to suppress them, they will first rebel and then, if we are successful in our essays at murder, will atrophy and decay, setting up a kind of spiritual blood-poisoning. A system of morality that results in blood-poisoning, and even idealizes the state of chronic blood-poisoning as the perfect life, is surely not the best that human ingenuity can devise. We are justified in preferring the morality which teaches the subjugation of the self to things as well as of things to the self, and which, in this way, guarantees not only social efficiency (for good citizenship is almost entirely a matter of subduing things to self), but also completeness and health of individual life.

La Fontaine has summed up the whole matter in one of the best of his fables—that of the two philosophical gardeners, the Greek and the Scythian.

The Greek prunes his trees for their good.

> J'ôte le superflu, dit l'autre ; et, l'abattant,
> Le reste en profite autant.

The Scythian returns to his *triste demeure* and sets himself to imitate his colleague. With what excess of zeal !

> Il ôte de chez lui les branches les plus belles
> Il tronque son verger contre toute raison . . .
> Tout languit et tout meurt.
>> Ce Scythe exprime bien
>> Un indiscret stoïcien :
>> Celui-ci retranche de l'âme
> Désirs et passions, le bon et le mauvais,
>> Jusqu'aux plus innocents souhaits
> Contre de telles gens, quant à moi, je réclame.
> Ils ôtent à nos cœurs le principal ressort ;
> Ils font cesser de vivre avant que l'on soit mort.

And by condemning us to a living death, he might have added, they condemn us also to a premature decay. Mortification of the flesh, in the religious sense of the term, results in a mortification of the soul that is only too distressingly medical—in a spiritual gangrene, a putrefaction, a stink.

The Khlysty principles have a more than merely ethical application. They are also of significance for the artist, both for the artist in life and for the professional creator. No man can live—richly and harmoniously live—no man can beautifully create, who does not sometimes subdue himself to things—to the unknown modes of being of the external world and of his own unconsciousness. Modern ' nature - worship ' springs from a recognition of this fact. ' Come forth,' said Wordsworth,

> Come forth, and bring with you a heart
> That watches and receives.

If he had always acted on his own advice, instead of coming forth with a heart full of Anglicanism and middle-class respectability, he would have been a better poet.

Nature-worship is a modern, artificial, and somewhat precarious invention of refined minds. Admirable, but somehow, in too many instances, rather ridiculous in being so refined, so rootlessly high-class. In the woods of Dorking, Meredith has the air of a whiskered Marie Antoinette, playing at being a shepherdess. The Greeks were not Wordsworthians or Meredithians ; they never went for walking tours nor wasted their energies unnecessarily climbing to the tops of mountains. Nevertheless, their religion kept them more intimately in touch with the alien world of external things and the (to the conscious will and intellect) hardly less alien inner world of instinctive and passional reactions to things, than all the high-class nature-worship of the moderns could have done. Their ritual put them into a direct physical and emotional relationship with the forces of nature—forces which their mythology had represented anthropomorphically, indeed, but in the likeness of man the darkly passionate and desirous being as well as in that of man the conscious, the spiritual, the intellectual. The modern nature-worshipper's God is apt to be visualized too exclusively as *homo sapiens*—and *sapiens* to the *n*th degree.

St. Francis is often hailed as the first nature-worshipper to appear in Europe since the time of the Greeks. It is a claim which the facts do not make good. Mediæval Europe was full of genuine nature-worshippers, and St. Francis was not one of them. The genuine nature-worshippers were the followers of that old, pre-Christian religion which lingered on through all the Middle Ages in the form of witchcraft and its elaborate organization, its traditional rites. A cult of fertility, the old religion existed to establish between the human soul and the souls of animals, of plants and places, of the seasons and the sun, a direct participative communion. The people who attended the Sabbaths were not sophisticated walking-tourers with high-class pantheistic feelings about the beauty spots of the Lake District. In spite of this, however, or perhaps because of it, they were better nature-worshippers than the best Wordsworthians of them all.

Francis lacked the advantages which he might have derived from a sound pagan upbringing among the sorcerers. His family was orthodoxly Christian. The ritual communion with things was unknown to him. Like Wordsworth, he had to invent his own nature-worship, to produce it by a sort of spiritual conjuring trick out of a vacuum. Reading his life, one sees that his conjuring trick only very imperfectly ' came off.' Inevitably. For Francis was not prepared to subjugate himself to things ; he utterly lacked the humility of those who can submit themselves passively, for a season, to alien influences ; he was too proudly wilful ever to allow his soul to participate in unknown modes of being.

Modern writers have praised him for his charming sympathy with animals. It is a praise, if we can credit the testimony of the original documents, most strangely misdirected. The fact that Francis called donkeys his brothers and bullfinches his sisters is not enough in itself to prove that he lived in any kind of fraternal communion with his adopted family. Let me quote, in this context, a story from the *Fioretti* of Brother Juniper, ' one of the most elect disciples . . . a man of great fervour and charity, of whom St. Francis said, " He would be a good Brother Minor, who had conquered himself and the world like Brother

Juniper." ' Here is the anecdote, a little abridged. ' On a time at St. Mary of the Angels, when, all afire with the love of God, he was visiting a sick brother, he asked him, with much compassion, " Can I do thee any service ? " Replied the sick man, " Much comfort would it give me, if thou couldst give me a pig's trotter to eat." Straightway cried Brother Juniper, " Leave that to me ; I 'll fetch thee one at once." So he went and took a knife and, in fervour of spirit, ran through the wood, where divers pigs were feeding, threw himself on one of them, cut off its foot and ran away, leaving the pig with feet so maimed ; and he washed and dressed and cooked the foot . . . and brought it to the sick man with much charity. And the sick man ate it up right greedily, to the great comfort and delight of Brother Juniper ; who, with great glee, for to glad the heart of this man, told him of the assault he had made on the pig. Meanwhile the swineherd had gone to tell his master *his* version of Brother Juniper's exploit ; who, when he had heard it, came in a great rage to the house of the Brothers and " called them hypocrites, thieves and liars, and rogues and knaves," saying, " Why have ye cut off the foot of my pig ? " St. Francis " with all humility made excuses " and " promised to restore all that he had lost." But for all that he was not appeased, but went away full of anger. St. Francis said within his heart, " Can Brother Juniper have done this thing, in zeal too indiscreet?"' Accordingly he questioned Juniper, who, 'not as one that had made a fault, but as one that seemed to himself to have done an act of great charity, all gladly answered and said : "Sweet my Father, it is true that I cut off a foot from the said pig. . . . And bearing in mind the consolation our sick brother felt, and the comfort that the said foot brought him, if I had cut off the feet of a hundred pigs as I did of one, in very sooth, methinks God would have said, Well done."' Upon which St. Francis rebuked him severely. ' " Oh Brother Juniper," he cried, "why hast thou given us so great a scandal? Not without reason does this man complain."' And he ordered the erring Brother to go and apologize to the pig-master. ' Brother Juniper was amazed that any one should be angry at so charitable a deed ; for it seemed to him that these temporal things were naught, save in so far as men in their charity shared them with their neighbours. "Why should he be so disquieted, seeing that this pig, whose foot I cut off, is rather God's than his?"' None the less, he did as he was told, sought out the pig-master and explained the matter 'with such charity and simplicity and humility, that this man, coming to himself again, threw himself on the ground, not without many tears ; and, acknowledging the wrong he had done and said unto the Brothers, went and caught the pig and killed it and, having cooked it, brought it with great

devotion and much weeping to St. Mary of the
Angels and gave it to the Brothers to eat, for
pity of the wrong he had done them. And St.
Francis, pondering on the simplicity and patience
of the said holy Brother Juniper in the hour of
trial, said to his companions and the others
standing round : " Would to God, my brothers,
that I had a whole forest of such Junipers ! " '

So ends the edifying story. It remains for us
to draw our conclusions from it. They will not,
I am afraid, be very favourable to St. Francis.
Brother Juniper, of course, could not have been
expected to know any better. All the anecdotes
about this personage paint him as a half-savage
zany entirely possessed, since his conversion, by
a single idea—the idea of Franciscan Christianity.
He was too much of an imbecile to see that there
could be anything in the bloody mutilation of a
defenceless animal incompatible with the purest
charity. To this clown and the doubtless equally
clownish Brother, whose longing for pig's trotters
was the *fons et origo* of the whole incident, the
maiming of the pig was not merely a commend-
able act of charity : it was also exquisitely
humorous. Juniper told the story ' with great
glee, for to glad the sick man's heart.' And
doubtless any half-witted rustic of the thirteenth
century would have whooped and roared with
laughter at the spectacle of a pig with only three
feet trailing a bleeding stump with squeals and
groans among the trees. But what of Francis ?

What of the man whom his modern biographers have slobbered over with a maudlin, vegetarian sentimentality as the first animal-lover, the prophet of nature-worship and humanitarianism? We find him rebuking the over-zealous Juniper —but not for hacking tit-bits off the living swine ; only for making a scandal, for getting the monks into trouble with the public. Of the pig and its bleeding stump of leg and its squealing in the wood he does not think at all. It never even occurs to him to tell his imbecile disciple that maiming pigs and leaving them to bleed is not a perfectly charitable act. On the contrary, he finds, when the scandal has been averted, that Juniper has behaved quite admirably. 'Would to God that I had a whole forest of such Junipers !' 'Amen,' responded his companions. But the pigs, strangely enough, were silent.

The truth is that Francis was never in any living, sympathetic contact with nature. He was too busily engaged in using his will power—on other people, in making them good ; on himself, in being ascetic and practising Christian humility —to be able to submit himself to the non-human influences from without and so participate in the alien life of things. In the sphere of pagan nature-worship Francis's wilful humility was a stiff-necked pride. He never really liked an animal, because he was never prepared to put himself, for a moment, in the animal's place. Indeed, the story of Brother Juniper's pig shows clearly that Francis was quite unconscious that there was a place to put himself into. The more famous, because more agreeable, story of his sermon to the birds forces on us the same conclusion. Reading it attentively, we perceive that he never really cared two pins for the birds as birds—as creatures, that is to say, entirely different from himself, leading an alien and refreshingly non-human life, about which, however, the human being can discover something by patient sympathy and humility. So far as we are concerned the whole 'point' of animals is that, in Whitman's words—

> They do not sweat and whine about their condition,
> They do not lie awake in the dark and weep for their sins,
> They do not make me sick discussing their duty to God,
> No one is dissatisfied, not one is demented with the mania of owning things,
> Not one kneels to another, nor to his kind that lived thousands of years ago,
> Not one is respectable or industrious over the whole earth.

Francis failed to realize this because, lacking the necessary humility, refusing to submit himself to things, he could never establish a sympathetic relationship with creatures whose mode of being was other than his own. He talked to the birds as though they were respectable and industrious Christians with tender consciences and a well-developed theology and a strong sense of their duty to God—to Francis's God, of course, and not the feathered deity of the farmyard and the copse.

Mr. Chesterton discovers evidence of St. Francis's exquisite feeling for nature in his apt attributions of sex—as of femininity to Sister Moon and maleness to Brother Sun, and so on. More philologically-minded writers, however, have found in these attributions nothing more than a tribute to Latin and Italian grammar. *Luna* is grammatically of the feminine gender ; what more obvious than to call the moon ' sister ' ? But let us admit for the sake of argument that the Saint had more than merely grammatical intentions in calling things by masculine and feminine names. The case against grammar is strongest in regard to the birds. These he addresses as his sisters, in spite of the fact that *uccello* is masculine—though it should be remembered that *avis*, in a possibly earlier Latin version of the *Fioretti*, is a feminine word. ' My little sisters, the birds.' Mr. Chesterton would doubtless applaud. But the drake and the cock-bullfinch, the sparrow, the gaudy pheasant, and the arrogantly strutting cock—how they would protest against the insult ! ' Call us your little sisters ? You might as well say : My little sisters, the officers of the Grenadier Guards.'

A man misses something by not establishing a participative and living relationship with the non-human world of animals and plants, landscapes and stars and seasons. By failing to be, vicariously, the not-self, he fails to be completely himself. There can be no complete integration of the soul without humility towards things as well as a will to subdue them. Those who lack that humility are bad artists in life.

They are also bad artists in art. For the creative arts, no less than the art of life, demand of their practitioners an alternation of contradictory activities—a subjugation of things to self and also of the self to things. The artists whose attitude to things is too passively humble are only half-creators. There is still an element of chaos in what they do ; the lumpy material in which they work still clings distortingly to the form they are trying to extract from it. They are either the slaves of appearances (like the feebler impressionists) ; or else, slaves of passion and feeling, they protest too much (as the feebler Elizabethans and romantics too much protested) and so fail utterly, in spite, or because, of their hysterical emotionalism, to create a moving work. For, by an apparent paradox, artists who abandon themselves too unreservedly to passion are unable to create passion—only its parody, or at the best a wild, grotesque extravagance. The history of literature shows that the extreme romantic style is suitable only for Gargantuan comedy, not tragedy ; for the delineation of enormous absurdity, not enormous passion.

The attempt artistically to present life in the

raw, so to speak, results almost invariably in the production of something lifeless. Things must to some extent be subdued to the generalizing, abstracting, rationalizing intellect ; otherwise the work of art, of which these things are the material, will lack substantiality and even—however faithfully direct impressions may be recorded—life. Examples of the lifelessness of works whose closeness to actuality might have been expected to give them vitality may be found in abundance. In their anxiety to catch the actual luminous appearance of things, the impressionists allowed all substantiality to evaporate from their creations ; the world in their pictures lost its body and died. Or take the case of the Goncourts in literature : it is when they transcribe most faithfully from their only too well-filled notebooks that their novels become most lifeless. As a contemporary example we may cite the work of Miss Dorothy Richardson. Her microscopic fidelity to the psychological facts defeats its own ends. Reduced to the elementary and atomic condition, her personages fade out of existence as integrated human beings. A similar fate has attended the creations of the Surréalistes. They have presented us, not with the finished product of creative thought, but with the dream-like incoherencies which creative thought uses as its raw material. It is the statue that lives, not the stone.

But if too much humility towards 'things' is fatal to art, so also is too much arrogance. To protest too little in the name of some moral or aesthetic stoicism is as bad as to protest too much. The art of those slaves of appearances who lack the force or the will to organize the chaos of immediate experience is always imperfect ; but not more so than the art of those who aspire to organize it too much, of those who are not content till they have substituted for nature's infinite variety, nature's quickness and vividness and softness, nature's sliding lines and subtly curving or arbitrarily broken surfaces, the metallic and rigorous simplicity of a few abstract geometrical forms. Whole epochs of literary and artistic history have been afflicted by the geometrizing mania. The French *Grand Siècle*, for example—an age, it is true, that produced genuinely grand works (for after all, if a man has a sufficiency of force and talent, he can create fine things out of the most unpromising materials and in the teeth of almost any resistance), but which might have produced yet grander ones if its aesthetic theory had not been so insistently haunted by the shade of Euclid. Geometry is doubtless an excellent thing ; but a well-composed landscape with figures is still better. At the present time literature is perhaps insufficiently geometrical. It protests too much ; it abandons itself too passively to appearances ; it is excessively interested in the raw material of thought and imagination, and not enough in the working up of that material into perfected forms. With contemporary painting, however, the case is different. Reacting against impressionism on the one hand and a conventionally realistic literariness on the other, the most self-consciously talented of modern painters deliberately transformed their art into a branch of geometry. The possibilities of cubism in its strictest form were, however, soon exhausted. There has been a general return to representation—but to a representation still much too arrogantly geometrical in its studied omissions and distortions. Art is still insufficiently humble before its subject-matter. Painters insist on subjecting the outer world too completely to their abstracting and geometrizing intellects. A kind of aesthetic asceticism prevents them from enjoying whole-heartedly and without afterthought the loveliness so profusely offered by the world about them. It is on principle that they subdue their feeling for nature, as a stoic or a monk subdues his passions. Tyrannically, they impose their will on things ; they substitute arbitrary forms of their own fabrication for the almost invariably much subtler and lovelier forms with which their direct experience presents them. The result, it seems to me, has been an impoverishment, a deadening of the art. There are welcome signs that the painters themselves are coming to the same conclusion. At any rate, they seem to be repenting a little of their asceticism ; they seem to be abating a little of their geometrician's arrogance ; they are cultivating a certain humility towards things. Old Renoir summed up the truth about painting in one oracular sentence. ' Un peintre, voyez-vous, qui a le sentiment des fesses et du téton, c'est un homme sauvé.' Saved—but by Grigory's ' salvation through sin,' by a subjugation of the self to things, by a total humility before that divine and mysterious nature, of which breasts and buttocks are but a part—though doubtless, from our all too human point of view, a peculiarly important part. For this ' sentiment des fesses et du téton ' is simply a special case of the sentiment of nature, and the embrace of consummated love is the communion of the self with the not-self, the Wordsworthian participation with unknown modes of being, in its most intense and completest form.

The artist, then, like the man, is saved through sin. But he is also saved through sinlessness—saved by the subjugation of things to self no less than by that of the self to things. Francis and Grigory are both right and both wrong. Each separately leads astray ; but together and in their mutual contradiction they are the best of guides.

# BAUDELAIRE

Inasmuch as he pursues an absolute, the absolute of evil, ' Le débauché est un grand philosophe.' (The *mot* is attributed to the moderately eminent French metaphysician, Jules Lachelier.) The debauchee is a great philosopher. As it stands, the assertion is a little too sweeping ; it needs qualification. No doubt, the debauchee *was* a great philosopher, once. But ever since the day of Hume he has ceased to be a great philosopher and become a rather silly one. For though it may be sublime to pursue the demonstrably unattainable, it is also ridiculous. A man may spend a laborious and ascetic lifetime writing books on the selenography of the back-side of the moon ; we may admire his single-mindedness (if single-mindedness happens to be a quality that strikes us as being admirable), but we must also laugh at his folly. To pursue the absolute is as demonstrably a waste of time as to speculate on the topography of the invisible portions of the moon. Inasmuch as he attempts to rationalize an absolute wickedness, the debauchee may be something of a heroic figure. But he is also something of a figure of fun. And as a philosopher he is, in spite of Professor Lachelier, silly.

Even the sublimest of the satanists are a little ridiculous. For they are mad, all mad ; and,

however tragical and appalling their insanity
may be, madmen are always ridiculous. Ridiculous in their enormous unawareness, in their
blindness, in the fixity of their moods, their iron
consistency, their unvarying reactions to all that
appeals to their mania. Ridiculous, in a word,
because they are inhuman. And similarly, even
the sublimest satanists (and with them, of course,
their looking-glass counterparts, the sublimest
saints) are ridiculous as well as grand, because
they share with the madman (and deliberately
share) his partial blindness, his stiffness, his
strained and focussed and unwavering fixity of
monomaniacal purpose, his inhumanity.

The contrary and at the same time the complement of inhuman rigidity and consistency is
a certain inhuman liberty. Concentrated on his
one idea, the madman is out of contact with
everything else. He loses all touch with reality,
and so is free from those limitations which the
necessity of making vital adjustments to the outside world imposes on the sane. In spite of their
rigid consistency of thought and action, or rather
because of it, the saint and the satanist are free,
like the madman, to disregard everything but
their fixed idea. Often this idea is of a kind
which prevents them from having anything like
the normal physical relationship with their
fellows and with the world at large. When this
happens, their inhuman liberty is complete,
manifest in all its ghastly grotesqueness. What

happens when the intellect and imagination are allowed to break away completely from the wholesome control of the body and the instincts is illustrated with incomparable power by Dostoievsky. Take, for example, *The Possessed*. In the whole of that extraordinary and horrible novel (and the same is true of all Dostoievsky's books) there is not one single character who has a decent physical relationship with any one or any thing whatsoever. Dostoievsky's people do not even eat normally, much less make love, or work, or enjoy nature. That would be much too easy and obvious for such parvenus of intelligence and consciousness as the Russians. Commonplace love, mere creative labour, vulgar enjoyment of real sensuous beauty—these are activities neither ' spiritual ' nor ' sinful ' enough for newly-conscious Christians, and altogether too ' irrational ' to satisfy ex-moujiks suddenly enriched with all the gradually accumulated cultural wealth of Europe. Dostoievsky's characters are typical Russian parvenus to consciousness. Unrestrained by the body, their intellect and imagination have become at once licentious and monomaniacal. And when at last they feel impelled to put their wild, unrestrained imaginings into practice—for it is impossible to go on staring at one's own navel without in the long-run becoming a trifle bored — what happens? They go and commit suicide, or murder, or rape, according to the turn their monomanias happen to have taken. How tragic it all is ! But also how stupid and grotesque ! If Stavrogin could have gone to bed with women he liked, instead of sleeping, on satanically ascetic principles, with women he detested ; if Kirillov had had a wife and a job of decent work ; if Pyotr Stepanovitch had ever looked with pleasure at a landscape or played with a kitten, —none of these tragedies, these fundamentally ludicrous and idiotic tragedies, would have taken place. The horrors that darken *The Possessed* and the other novels of Dostoievsky are tragedies of mental licentiousness. All Dostoievsky's characters (and Dostoievsky himself, one suspects, was rather like them) have licentious minds, utterly unrestrained by their bodies. They are all emotional onanists, wildly indulging themselves in the void of imagination. Occasionally they grow tired of their masturbations and try to make contact with the world. But they have lost all sense of reality, all knowledge of human values. All their attempts to realize their onanistic dreaming in practice result in catastrophe. It is inevitable. But however agonizing they may be (and Dostoievsky spares us nothing), these tragedies, I repeat, are fundamentally ludicrous and idiotic. They are the absurdly unnecessary tragedies of self-made madmen. We suffer in sympathy, but against our will ; afterwards we must laugh. For these tragedies are nothing but stupid farces that have been carried too far.

Robert Burns, after Chaucer the least preten-
tious and portentous, the most completely and
harmoniously human of all English poets, understood this well. His ' Address to the Deil ' has
for epigraph two tremendous lines from *Paradise
Lost* :

> O Prince ! O Chief of many thronèd pow'rs
> That led th' embattled Seraphim to war !

The words go rumbling through the spaces of
the Miltonic universe, reverberate in fearful
thunder from the roof of hell, in solemn and
celestial music from sphere after crystal sphere ;
but when at last they strike the earth, what very
strange and even indecorous echoes are returned !

> O Thou ! whatever title suit thee,
> Auld Hornie, Satan, Nick, or Clootie,
> Wha in yon cavern grim and sootie,
>     Closed under hatches,
> Spairges about the brunstane cootie,
>     To scaud poor wretches !

It is the voice of humanity, of sane and humorous and unpretentious humanity, that speaks.
Larger than life and half as natural, Milton
declaims the potent charms that call up Satan
from the abyss ; saint and fiend, they stand
together, a pair of twins. They are sublime,
but for that very reason ridiculous. For the
Chief of many thronèd powers is also a comic
character, grotesque, like some too villainous

villain in an old melodrama—like some too
virtuous hero, for that matter.

And the lesser satanists are like their masters.
Don Juan, Cain, Heathcliff, Stavrogin—they are
all of them figures of fun, in spite of their
sublimity, or rather because of it. And the
satanists of real life are almost as ridiculous as
the satanists of literature. Almost ; but not
quite, because, unless he is stark, staring mad, the
living satanist is never so stiffly consistent, never
so utterly free from the normal human restraints,
as the satanist in books. It is only when satanists
fail to live up to the satanic character that
we can take them seriously—for it is then that
they begin to be human. When they sublimely
succeed, we are compelled to laugh. ' Laughter,'
said Baudelaire, ' is satanic.' Some laughter,
perhaps. But by no means all. There is a
whole gamut of humorous and unferocious
laughter that is entirely and characteristically
human. And I suspect that it was precisely this
human laughter that Baudelaire, the satanist,
described as satanic. His values were reversed.
The mirth which men like Chaucer or Burns
would have found friendly in its quality of
humanness, Baudelaire necessarily found hostile
and fiendish. For if the devil is man's worst
enemy, man is also the devil's. The most powerful solvent of satanic as of any other superhuman pretentions is the good-humoured
laughter of human beings. Call the devil Nick

or Auld Hornie, and he loses immediately all his impressiveness and half his formidableness. Hence Baudelaire's hatred of laughter ; from his satanic point of view it was indeed diabolical. Satan must be dignified at all costs. In his superb and portentous carapace there must be no chink through which the shafts of men's mirth can enter. The laughter-proof armour in which Baudelaire passed his life was a 'sober dandyism' of dress, a frigidly aristocratic manner, a more than English coldness. His clothes, according to Théophile Gautier, had 'un cachet voulu de simplicité anglaise et comme l'intention de se séparer du genre artiste.' 'Contrairement aux mœurs un peu débraillées des artistes, Baudelaire se piquait de garder les plus étroites convenances, et sa politesse était excessive jusqu'à paraître maniérée. Il mesurait ses phrases, n'employait que les termes les plus choisis. . . . La charge, très en honneur à Pimodan, était dédaignée par lui comme artiste et grossière ; mais il ne s'interdisait pas le paradoxe et l'outrance. D'un air très simple, très naturel et parfaitement détaché . . . il avançait quelque axiome satanique monstrueux. Ses gestes étaient lents, rares et sobres, rapprochés du corps, car il avait en horreur la gesticulation méridionale. Il n'aimait pas non plus la volubilité de parole, et la froideur britannique lui semblait de bon goût. On peut dire de lui que c'était un dandy égaré dans la bohème mais y gardant son rang et ses manières et ce culte de soi-même qui caractérise l'homme imbu des principes de Brummell.' What elaborate precautions against the possible laughter of humanity ! Satan is a gentleman, and only on condition of remaining a gentleman can he be Satan. The moment he loses his Brummellesque dignity and becomes Auld Hornie or Auld Nick, he is just a poor devil, nothing more. If Baudelaire could sometimes have dropped his dandy's correctness, could sometimes have permitted himself to be called Clootie, he would have been certainly a happier and completer man and perhaps a better because a more comprehensive poet.

But he preferred to cling to his satanic dignity ; he buckled his laughter-proof armour yet more tightly about him  It was as a kind of Black Prince that he confronted the world—a dark figure, tragical and terrific, but at the same time ludicrous in being too imposing, insufficiently supple.

'Sin,' says St. Paul, 'is not imputed when there is no law. . . . Moreover, the law entered, that the offence might abound.' Only a believer in absolute goodness can consciously pursue the absolute of evil ; you cannot be a Satanist without being at the same time, potentially or actually, a Godist. Baudelaire was a Christian inside out, the photographic image in negative of a Father of the Church. His philosophy was orthodox—nay, more than orthodox, almost jansenistic. His views on original sin (in modern times the touchstone of orthodoxy) were entirely sound. They were much sounder, for example, than those of Jesus. Jesus could say, speaking of little children, that ' of such is the kingdom of heaven ' ; a sound Augustinian, Baudelaire called them ' des Satans en herbe.' He had the good Christian's contempt for the modern belief in progress. ' La croyance au progrès,' he said, ' est une doctrine de Belges.' And when Baudelaire had said of a thing that it was Belgian he had called it the worst name in his vocabulary.

To this Christian, who accepted the doctrine of the Fall with all its consequences, Humanitarianism was simply criminal nonsense. Man was by nature malignant and stupid. The ' universal silliness of every class, individual, sex, and age ' filled him, as it filled Flaubert, with a chronic indignation. Those who, like the painter Wiertz (another Belgian !), believed in ' the immortal principles of '89,' he regarded almost as personal enemies. ' Le Christ des humanitaires,' he writes in his notes on Wiertz. ' Peinture philosophique. Sottises analogues à celles de Victor Hugo à la fin des Contemplations. Abolition de la peine de mort, puissance infinie de l'homme ! ' For the democrat's ingenuous faith in the power of education to make all men equally intelligent and virtuous he had nothing but contempt. One of his projects was to write an essay on the 'infamie de l'imprimerie, grand obstacle au développement du Beau.' Wholly Christian again was Baudelaire's attitude towards the question of individual responsibility. For the eighteenth-century humanitarians, who started from the axiom that man in a 'state of nature' is virtuous and reasonable, there could not, logically, be such a thing as sin in the Christian, or crime in the legal, sense of the word ; the individual was not to blame for his bad actions. The entire responsibility rested with the Environment, with Society, with Bad Laws, Priestcraft, Superstition, and so forth. For Baudelaire only the individual counted. Those who do wrong must bear the whole responsibility for their wrongdoing. And what actions, according to Baudelaire, are wrong ? The answer is simple : they are the actions which the Church regards as sinful. St. Paul never hated the flesh and all its works more venomously than did Baudelaire ; Prudentius never wrote of love with a fiercer vehemence of disgust. For the poet, as for the Christian moralists, the worst, because the most attractive, the commonest, the apparently most harmless sins were those of a sexual nature. Avoid them, then ! was the command of the moralists. But Baudelaire was a looking-glass Christian ; for him the categorical imperative was just the opposite of this. Indulgence is hateful to God ; therefore (such is the logic of the satanists) indulge. 'La volupté unique

et suprême de l'amour gît dans la certitude de
faire le mal. Et l'homme et la femme savent de
naissance que dans le mal se trouve toute volupté.'
Baudelaire liked revolution for the same reason
as he liked love. 'Moi, quand je consens à être
républicain' (he did a little desultory shooting
from the barricades in 1848), 'je fais le mal, le
sachant. . . . Je dis : Vive la Révolution ! comme
je dirais : Vive la Destruction ! Vive la Mort !
Nous avons tous l'esprit républicain dans les
veines comme la vérole dans les os. Nous sommes
démocratisés et syphilisés !' He hated and
despised the revolutionaries who imagined that
they were acting for the benefit of the human
race. 'Moi, je me fous du genre humain.' 'A
taste for vengeance and the natural pleasure
of demolition' were what drove *him* to the
barricades.

But politics and, in general, 'action' (in the
popular sense of the word) were distasteful to
him. It was only theoretically that he 'understood a man's deserting one cause for the sake
of knowing what it would feel like to serve
another.' An invincible dislike of all causes but
that of poetry prevented him from attempting
the experiment in practice. And in the same
way, when he said that 'not only would he be
happy to be the victim, but that he would not
object to being the executioner—so as to
feel the Revolution in both ways,' it was only
a matter of words. His own active participa-

tion in the Revolution was too brief to permit of his being either victim or executioner.

Much of Baudelaire's satanism even outside the sphere of politics was confined to words. Inevitably : for Baudelaire liked his freedom, and in a well-policed society the satanists who put their principles too freely into practice get thrown into gaol. From Baudelaire's conversation you would have imagined that he was a mixture of Gilles de Rais, Heliogabalus, and the Marquis de Sade. At any rate, that was what he wanted you to imagine. But reputations have a strange life of their own, over which their subject has little or no control. Baudelaire would have liked the world to regard him as the incarnation of all the gentlemanly wickednesses. Instead of which—but let me quote his own words : ' Un jour une femme me dit : C'est singulier ; vous êtes fort convenable ; je croyais que vous étiez toujours ivre et que vous sentiez mauvais.'

To have the reputation of being unpleasantly smelly—could anything have been more humiliating to the man who saw himself as the Chief of many thronèd powers ! Those who knew him personally made, of course, no such mistakes. Their friend was no vulgar Bohemian, but a Dandy ; if he was wicked, it was in the grand manner, like a gentleman, not an artist. But they also knew that a great deal of his aristocratic satanism was purely platonic and conversational. Baudelaire was a practising satanist only in those circumstances in which active satanism is not interfered with by the police. All satanisms of violence and fraud were thus ruled out. He talked about treacheries and executions, but did not act them. The most interesting of the legally tolerated sins are those of the flesh. Baudelaire was therefore, above all, a satanist of love. But not in the manner of the ferocious Marquis, nor even of Don Juan. He did not victimize his partners ; he victimized only himself. His cruelties were directed inwards. Harmlessly, one is tempted to say ; the harmless cruelties of an academic satanist. And harmless, in one sense, they were. Baudelaire's path was not strewn with seduced young girls, adulterous wives, and flagellated actresses. Regrettably, perhaps. For this apparently harmless variety of satanism is in certain ways the most harmful of all. The flagellator and the seducer do a certain strictly limited amount of damage among their feminine acquaintances. The self-victimizing satanist is infinitely more destructive. For what are a few virginities and a few square inches of tanned cocotte-skin compared with the entire universe ? The entire universe—nothing less. The satanist who is his own victim defaces and defiles for himself the entire universe. And when, like Baudelaire, he happens to be a great poet, he defaces and defiles it for his readers. Your Sades and

Juans are never ruinous on this enormous scale
For they enjoy their satanisms—not very
whole-heartedly, perhaps, and always crazily
but still enjoy. They go their way carolling
with Pippa : ' Nick's in his Hades, all's right with
the world.' The self-victimizer has no enjoy-
ments to rationalize into a jolly Browningesque
philosophy. The world is hateful to him ; he
himself has made it so.

Baudelaire treated himself with a studied
malignancy. He took pains to make the world
as thoroughly disgusting for himself as he could
As an example of his satanic technique, let me
quote this fragment of autobiography from one
of his sonnets :

> Une nuit que j'étais près d'une affreuse juive,
>   Comme au long d'un cadavre un cadavre étendu
>   Je me pris à songer près de ce corps vendu
> A la triste beauté dont mon désir se prive.

Appalling lines ! Reading them, one seems to
sink through layer after darkening, thickening
layer of slimy horror. A shuddering pity takes
hold of one. And then amazement, amazement
at the thought that this revolting torture was
self-inflicted.

Torture, torture—the word comes back to
one hauntingly, again and again, as one reads
the *Fleurs du Mal*. Baudelaire himself brooded
over the notion. ' Love is like a torture or a
surgical operation. This idea can be developed

184

in the bitterest way. Even when the two lovers
are very much in love and full of reciprocal
desires, one of the two will always be calmer
or less possessed than the other. He, or she, is
the operator, the executioner ; the other is the
patient, the victim.' The tortures which Baudelaire inflicted on himself were not mere operations ; they were more horrible than that.
Between him and the 'frightful Jewesses' there
was not even the possibility of reciprocal desire
—there was nothing but disgust. His tortures were mostly those of defilement. To be
chained to a corpse, to be confined in the midst
of rats and excrement—these were the punish-
ments to which he satanically condemned himself.
And even his respites from the frightful Jewesses
were only milder tortures. That 'sad beauty of
whom his desire deprived itself' was a drunken
negress, whose vulgarity shocked every fibre of
his soul, whose stupidity amazed and appalled
him, who drained him of his money and showed
her gratitude by cuckolding him whenever she
had an opportunity.

Quand elle eut de mes os sucé toute la moelle,
Et que languissamment je me tournai vers elle
Pour lui rendre un baiser d'amour, je ne vis plus
Qu'une outre aux flancs gluants, toute pleine de
pus.

In spite of which, or because of which, Baudelaire remained indissolubly attached to his

mulatto. After their most serious quarrel he lay in his bed for days, uncontrollably and incessantly weeping. In spite or because of the fact that she represented sex in its lowest form, he loved her.

But frightful Jewesses and hardly less frightful negresses were not the only object of Baudelaire's love. For,

> Quand chez les débauchés l'aube blanche et vermeille
>   Entre en société de l'Idéal rongeur,
>   Par l'opération d'un mystère vengeur
> Dans la brute assoupie un ange se réveille.

In other words, that morning-after sentiment, that *omne-animal-triste* feeling which, according to the Ancients, tinges with melancholy the loves of every creature but the mare and the woman, is easily and naturally rationalized in terms of Christian-Platonic idealism. The angel in Baudelaire was never fast asleep. For, as I have already pointed out, a man cannot be a Satanist who is not at the same time a Godist. Above the frightful Jewesses and negresses among whom Baudelaire had condemned himself to pass his life, hovered a white-winged, white-night-gowned ideal of feminine purity. The lineaments of this angelic child of fancy were by the poet occasionally superimposed on those of a real, flesh-and-blood woman, who thereupon ceased to be a woman and became, in the words used by Baudelaire himself when writing to one of his deified lady friends (an artist's model in this case), ' un objet de culte ' which it was ' impossible de souiller.' Unhappily the ' impossibility of defilement ' was not so absolute as he could have wished. Idealization is a process which takes place only in the idealist's fancy : it has no perceptible effect upon the thing idealized. The ' object of worship ' remains incurably what it was—in this case a woman. This regrettable fact was personally rediscovered by Baudelaire in the most ridiculously humiliating circumstances. Mme. Sabatier was a merry young widow who gave literary and artistic dinner-parties. The Goncourts call her ' une vivandière de faunes ' ; and she herself, it would seem, was also a trifle faunesque in her tastes and habits. It was in this unlikely temple of plump luxuriant flesh and more than ordinarily warm blood that Baudelaire chose to lodge his divine ideal. The fauns' barmaid became for him an object of worship. For five years he adored, piously. Then, the publication of the *Fleurs du Mal* and the subsequent lawsuit having made him suddenly famous, Mme. Sabatier decided, without solicitation on his part, to yield. Invited to treat his deity as a human, even an all too human being, Baudelaire found himself incapable of rising to the occasion. The lady was offended—justifiably. She reproached him. Baudelaire re-

turned her reproaches. 'Il y a quelques jours,'
he wrote, 'tu étais une divinité, ce qui est si
commode, ce qui est si beau, ce qui est si inviolable. Te voilà femme maintenant.' It was
unforgivable. 'J'ai horreur de la passion,' he
went on to explain, 'parce que je la connais
avec toutes ses ignominies.' As a matter of
fact, Baudelaire knew very little about passion.
He knew the defiling torture of submitting to
the embraces of frightful Jewesses; and, in
the arms of his negress, he knew the madness,
the fixed incurable monomania, of exclusive
sensuality. At the other end of the scale he
knew the worship of inviolable divinities—a
worship, of which one of the conditions was
precisely the joyless or frantic debauchery
among the Jewesses and negresses. For 'la
femme dont on ne jouit point est celle qu'on
aime. . . . Ce qui rend la maîtresse plus chère,
c'est la débauche avec d'autres femmes. Ce
qu'elle perd en jouissances sensuelles elle gagne
en adoration.' These strange perversities were
what Baudelaire called passion. Of the more
normal amorous relationships he was wholly
ignorant. We may doubt whether he ever
embraced a woman he respected, or knew what
it was to combine desire with esteem, and tenderness with passion. Indeed, he would have
denied the very possibility of such combina-
tions. His theory of love was the theory of
those extreme, almost Manichean Christians

who condemned indiscriminately every form of physical passion, and regarded even marriage as a sin. Between mind and body, spirit and matter, he had fixed an impassable gulf. Body was wholly bad ; therefore, according to the logic of satanism, it had to be indulged as much and above all as sordidly as possible. Spirit was wholly good ; therefore, when ' dans la brute assoupie un ange se réveille,' there must be nothing in the nature of a (by definition) defiling physical contact.

Where love was concerned, Baudelaire, in the phrase of Ivan Karamazov, ' returned God his entrance ticket.' He refused to accept love ; he wanted something better. With the result, of course, that he got something much worse and that love refused to accept *him*. The best is ever the enemy of the good, and nowhere more murderously the enemy than where love is concerned. Baudelaire's idea of the best love was a purely mental relationship, a conscious interbecoming of two hitherto separate beings. Ordinary, unideal love was for him an ' épouvantable jeu,' because at least ' one of the players must lose the government of himself.' Moreover, ' dans l'amour, comme dans presque toutes les affaires humaines, l'entente cordiale est le résultat d'un malentendu. Ce malentendu, c'est le plaisir. L'homme crie : O mon ange ! La femme roucoule : Maman ! Maman ! Et ces deux imbéciles sont persuadés qu'ils pen-

sent de concert. Le gouffre infranchissable qui
fait l'incommunicabilité reste infranchi.' But,
after all, why shouldn't it remain uncrossed?
And why shouldn't one sometimes lose the
government of oneself? We may think ourselves happy that we do not possess a perfect
and uninterrupted awareness of self and of
others. How fatiguing existence would be
if consciousness and will were never given a
holiday, if there were no 'frightful games,'
in the course of which one might occasionally lose one's head! How fatiguing! And
also how trivial and petty! For, in love at
any rate, a man loses his head for the sake
of something bigger and more important than
his own ego, of something not himself that
makes for life. And then the horror of being
wholly transparent to somebody else, wholly
clear-sighted oneself! Thanks, however, to
the body, there can be no complete awareness,
because there can be no mingling of substance,
no interbecoming. The body guarantees our
privacy, that inmost privacy, which we must
not attempt to violate under pain of betraying
our manhood.

> Aye free, aff han' your story tell,
>   When wi' a bosom cronie;
> But still keep something to yoursel'
>   Ye scarcely tell to onie.

To none, indeed—even in love. The realization of Baudelaire's ideal would be a psychological catastrophe. But being a sound, if satanic, Christian, with a prejudice in favour of mind and spirit, and a contemptuous hatred of the body, Baudelaire could not understand this ; on the contrary, he imagined that he was yearning for his own and humanity's highest good. When he saw that there was no prospect of his getting what he yearned for, he renounced love altogether in favour of self-tormenting debauchery on the one hand, and long-range adoration on the other.

With that sovereign good sense which, in spite of the strangenesses and absurdities of their beliefs, generally distinguished the actions of the men of the Middle Ages, the great platonizing poets of the thirteenth and fourteenth centuries harmonized philosophy and the exigencies of daily living, the ideal and the real, in a manner incomparably more satisfactory. Thus, there was a Mrs. Dante as well as a Beatrice, there were no less than four little Dantes ; Dante's friend and fellow-poet, Guido Cavalcanti, also had a wife and a family ; and though Petrarch never married, two bastard children, borne by the same mother and at an interval of six years, testify to the fact that Laura's inordinately platonic friend was only prevented by the accident of his having taken orders from being as good and faithful a husband as he was, by all accounts, a tenderly solicitous father. Admirably inconsistent, these poets sang the praises of sacred love, while making the very best of the profane variety in the arms of an esteemed and affectionate spouse. Their platonic relationships existed on the margin of marriage or its equivalent, just as, in the larger world, the monasteries existed on the margin of secular life. Monk and platonic mistress testified to the existence of the spiritual ideal ; those whose temperament impelled them to take extreme courses were at liberty to devote themselves to the ideal either in the cloister or in the poet's study. Whatever happened, the ideal was not to be allowed to invade the sanctities of normal domestic life. This, as we realize when we read the *Canterbury Tales* and the *Decameron*, remained throughout the Middle Ages most wholesomely pagan, in spite of Christianity. The Reformation upset the mediæval balance. Stupidly consistent, the Bible-reading Protestants abolished the monasteries and let loose the idealism, hitherto safely bottled up on the outskirts of normal life, on the devoted heads of ordinary men and women. For the monk was substituted the puritan. It was a change deplorably for the worse. Confined to his private asylum on the margin of society, the monk had been harmless. The puritan was free to range the world, blighting and persecuting as he went, free to make life poisonous, not only for himself, but for all who came near him. The puritan was and is a social danger, a public and private nuisance of the most odious kind. Baudelaire was a puritan inside out. Instead of asceticism and respectability he practised debauchery. The means he used were the opposite of those employed by the puritans ; but his motives and theirs, the ends that he and they achieved, were the same. He hated life as much as they did, and was as successful in destroying it.

Incapable of understanding the inconsistencies even of the mediæval Christians, Baudelaire was still less capable of understanding the much more radical inconsistencies of the pagan Greeks. For the Greeks, all the Gods (or in other words all the aspects of human nature) were equally divine. The art of life consisted, for them, in giving every God his due. These dues were various. Thus, Apollo's due was very different from the debt a man owed to Dionysus. Indeed, one due might be incompatible with another ; but every one was owed and, in its proper time and season, must be acknowledged. No God must be cheated and none overpaid. Baudelaire was utterly un-Hellenic. Only once or twice in all his work does he touch a pagan theme, and then it is as a puritanical Jansenist, as an early Father of the Church, that he treats it. Read, for example, the poem called 'Lesbos.' Here are a few characteristic extracts :

Laisse du vieux Platon se froncer l'œil austère ;
Tu tires ton pardon de l'excès des baisers . . .

Tu tires ton pardon de l'éternel martyre
Infligé sans relâche aux cœurs ambitieux . . .

Qui des Dieux osera, Lesbos, être ton juge,
   Et condamner ton front pâli dans les travaux,
Si ses balances d'or n'ont pesé le déluge,
   Des larmes qu'à la mer ont versé tes ruisseaux ?
Qui des Dieux osera, Lesbos, être ton juge ?

To the contemporaries and the successors of
Sappho these lines would have been absolutely
incomprehensible. All this talk about pardon
and martyrdom, judgment and tears — the
Greeks would have shaken their heads over it
in utter bewilderment. For them, love-making
was not something that required pardoning or
judging. And what did it matter, after all, if
' les Phyrnés l'une l'autre s'attirent ' ? To the
Greeks it was a matter of almost perfect indifference whether one made love with somebody of
one's own or somebody of the other sex. There
is little in Plato's writing and still less in the
reputation he enjoyed among his fellow-Greeks
to make us suppose that he frowned very
austerely on homosexual embraces. The Gods,
if one can credit their official biographers, were
as little likely to pass judgment on Lesbos as
Plato. And if one of them had taken it into
his head to do so, is it likely that he would
have found many tears in the Lesbian streams ?

None certainly of remorse or conscious guilt. The only tears which Hellenic lovers ever seem to have dropped were those, in youth, of unsatisfied desire and those, when age had made them feeble and ugly, of regret for pleasures irrevocably past. Occasionally, too, they may have wept the *lacrimae rerum*. For, like all realists, the Greeks were, at bottom, profoundly pessimistic. In spite of its beauty, its inexhaustible strangeness and rich diversity, the world, they perceived, is finally deplorable. Fate has no pity ; old age and death lie in wait at the end of every vista. It is therefore our duty to make the best of the world and its loveliness while we can—at any rate during the years of youth and strength. Hedonism is the natural companion of pessimism. Where there is laughter, there also you may expect to find the ' tears of things.' But as for tears of repentance and remorse—who but a fool would want to make the world more deplorable than it already is ? who but a life-hating criminal would want to increase the sum of misery at the expense of man's small portion of precarious joy ?

\*     \*     \*     \*     \*

The earth is rich in silicon ; but our bodies contain hardly a trace of it. It is poor in phosphorus ; yet in phosphorus we are rich. Sea water contains little lime and almost infinitely little copper ; nevertheless, there is copper in the blood of certain crustaceans and in the shell of every mollusc abundance of lime. It is much the same in the psychological as in the physical world. We live in a spiritual environment in which, at any given moment, certain ideas and sentiments abound, certain others are rare. But in any individual mind the proportions may be reversed. For the environment does not flow into us mechanically ; the living mind takes up from it only what suits it, or what it is capable of taking. What suits the majority of minds (which are but weak, under-organized beings) is of course the environment. But strong, original minds may and often do dislike their surroundings. What suits them may exist in only the smallest quantities in the spiritual medium they inhabit. But like the copper-blooded crustaceans, like the lime-shelled molluscs, they have a wonderful art to find and take up what they need. Baudelaire exemplifies this type. In the age of Buckle and Podsnap, of optimism and respectability, he was the most savage and gloomy of Augustinian Christians, the most conscientious of debauchees. Why ? His private history provides the explanation. The key facts are these : he had a childish passion for his mother, and his mother, while he was still a boy, married a second husband. This marriage was a shock from which he never recovered. Whole tracts of his consciousness were suddenly ravaged by it. He had adored and idealized—the more extravagantly for the fact that his adoration and idealization had been mingled with a precocious and slightly perverse sensuality. The divinity was suddenly thrown down and violated. He hated the violator and everything that could remind him of the act of violation ; he adored the memory of the yet inviolate divinity. The cynicism and perversity of adolescence got mixed in his hatred and made him take an agonizing and degrading pleasure in rehearsing in thought and, later, in act the scenes of violation. In the intervals, when he was exhausted, he worshipped a disembodied goddess. And this was what he went on doing all his life. Needing, like all men, a philosophical explanation for his actions, he found it in the semi-Manichean Christianity of the early monks and the Jansenists. A very slight twist was enough to turn the creed and ethics of Pascal into a self-torturing, world-destroying satanism. On the other face of the satanic medal were those tendencies towards 'spiritual' love, so grotesquely exemplified in the case of Mme. Sabatier.

Baudelaire was not merely a satanist ; he was a bored satanist. He was the poet of ennui, of that appalling boredom which can assume ' les proportions de l'immortalité.' The personal causes of this boredom are easily traceable. From quite early youth Baudelaire never enjoyed good health. Syphilis was in his blood : he drank too much ; he took, in one form or another, large quantities of opium ; he was an experimenter with haschisch ; he was chronically exhausted by a joyless and at last utterly pleasureless debauchery. In the physical circumstances it was difficult for a man to feel very gay and buoyant. His purse was as sick as his body. He was never out of debt ; his creditors unceasingly harassed him ; he lived in a perpetual state of anxiety. A neurosis of which one of the symptoms was a terrible depression was the result. This depression, he records, became almost unbearable during the autumn months — those terrible, dreary months—

Quand le ciel bas et lourd pèse comme un couvercle
   Sur l'esprit gémissant en proie aux longs ennuis,
Et que de l'horizon embrassant tout le cercle
   Il nous verse un jour noir plus triste que les nuits.

These are, I know, but summary and superficial generalizations ; and though it would be easy, with the aid of the biographical documents which the labours of the Crépets, father and son, have placed at our disposal, to explain, in detail and plausibly enough, all the characteristic features of Baudelaire's poetry in terms of his personal history, I shall not attempt the task. For what above all interests me here is not Baudelaire as a man, but Baudelaire as an influence, a persisting force. For a force he is.

‘ Avec Baudelaire,’ writes M. Paul Valéry,

'la poésie française sort enfin des frontières de la nation. Elle se fait lire dans le monde ; elle s'impose comme la poésie même de la modernité ; elle engendre l'imitation, elle féconde de nombreux esprits. . . . Je puis donc dire que, s'il est parmi nos poètes, des poètes plus grands et plus puissamment doués que Baudelaire, il n'en est de plus *important*.'

Baudelaire is now the most important of French, and indeed of European, poets. His poetry, which is the poetry of self-stultifying, world-destroying satanism and unutterable ennui, has come to be regarded 'comme la poésie même de la modernité.' The fact is, surely, odd. Let us try to understand its significance.

The most important of modern poets was a satanist. Does this mean that his contemporary admirers are, like him, despairing absolute-hunters with a

goût de l'infini
Qui partout dans le mal lui-même se proclame ?

No. For to be a Satanist, as I have said before, one must also be a Godist ; and the present age is singularly Godless. Debauchery was a tragical affair in Baudelaire's day ; it is now a merely medical one. We feel scientifically about our sins, not satanically. Why, then, do we admire this topsy-turvy Jansenist, for whom the only pleasure in love was the consciousness of doing wrong ? We ought to despise

him for being so hopelessly old-fashioned. And
hopelessly old-fashioned we do find him; but
only in the Christian and tragical interpretation of his actions. The actions themselves are
perfectly up-to-date. 'Tes débauches sans soif
et tes amours sans âme' are indistinguishable
from the extreme forms of the modern 'Good
Time.' The joylessness of modern pleasures
and modern love (which are, of course, the
image of the 'modern' pleasures and loves
of imperial Rome as it approached its catastrophe) is even completer than the joylessness
of Baudelaire's debauchery. For Baudelaire, the
Christian satanist, had at least the stimulating
consciousness that, in malignantly ruining the
universe for himself, he was doing evil. The
moderns fail to get even this 'kick' out of
their self- and world-destroying entertainments.
They perversely do what they don't want to
do, what fails to amuse them, and do not even
have the pleasure of imagining that they are
thereby committing a sin.

The flesh is diabolic, the spirit divine. Therefore, commands the satanist, indulge the flesh
to satiety and beyond. The modernist philosophy and the modernist ethic are different.
Neither the spirit nor the flesh, nor for that
matter anything at all, is divine. The only
important thing is that a man should be socially
efficient. Passion is the enemy of efficiency.
So don't let your instincts run away with you;

on the other hand, don't repress them too much. Repression interferes with efficiency. Efficiency demands that you should neither give yourself completely away nor keep yourself completely back. Those who live by this god-less philosophy and obey these purely medical commandments soon reduce their own lives and, consequently, the entire universe to a grey nothingness. In order not to be too unbearably conscious of this fact they surround themselves with an ever-increasing number of substitutes for genuine feeling. To create in themselves the illusion of being alive, they make a noise, they rush about, they hasten from distraction to distraction. Much to the profit of the shareholders in the great amusement industries. In a word, they have a Good Time.

Now, the better the time (in the modern sense of the term), the greater the boredom. Rivers found that the unhappy Melanesians literally and physically died of ennui when they were brought too suddenly in contact with modern amusements. We have grown gradually accustomed to the disease, and we therefore find it less lethal than do the South Sea islanders. We do not die outright of it ; it is only gradually that we approach the fatal conclusion of the malady. It will come, that fatal conclusion, when men have entirely lost the art of amusing themselves ; they will then simply perish of ennui. Modern creation-saving machinery has already begun to deprive them of this art. The progress of invention may confidently be expected to quicken the process. A few more triumphs in the style of the radio and the talkies, and the boredom which is now a mere discomfort will become an intolerable agony.

We turn to poetry for the perfect expression of our own feelings. In the *Fleurs du Mal* the modern finds all his own sufferings described —with what incomparable energy, in forms how memorably beautiful !

> Je suis comme le roi d'un pays pluvieux,
> Riche mais impuissant, jeune et pourtant très vieux !

It is ' la poésie même de la modernité.'

# HOLY FACE

Good Times are chronic nowadays. There is dancing every afternoon, a continuous performance at all the picture-palaces, a radio concert on tap, like gas or water, at any hour of the day or night. The fine point of seldom pleasure is duly blunted. Feasts must be solemn and rare, or else they cease to be feasts. 'Like stones of worth they thinly placed are' (or, at any rate, they were in Shakespeare's day, which was the day of Merry England), 'or captain jewels in the carconet.' The ghosts of these grand occasional jollifications still haunt our modern year. But the stones of worth are indistinguishable from the loud imitation jewellery which now adorns the entire circlet of days. Gems, when they are too large and too numerous, lose all their precious significance ; the treasure of an Indian prince is as unimpressive as Aladdin's cave at the pantomime. Set in the midst of the stage diamonds and rubies of modern pleasure, the old feasts are hardly visible. It is only among more or less completely rustic populations, lacking the means and the opportunity to indulge in the modern chronic Good Time, that the surviving feasts preserve something of their ancient glory. Me personally the unflagging pleasures of contemporary cities leave most lugubriously unamused. The prevailing boredom—for oh, how desperately bored, in spite of their grim determination to have a Good Time, the majority of pleasure-seekers really are !—the hopeless weariness, infect me. Among the lights, the alcohol, the hideous jazz noises, and the incessant movement I feel myself sinking into deeper and ever deeper despondency. By comparison with a night-club, churches are positively gay. If ever I want to make merry in public, I go where merry-making is occasional and the merriment, therefore, of genuine quality ; I go where feasts come rarely.

For one who would frequent only the occasional festivities, the great difficulty is to be in the right place at the right time. I have travelled through Belgium and found, in little market towns, kermesses that were orgiastic like the merry-making in a Breughel picture. But how to remember the date ? And how, remembering it, to be in Flanders again at the appointed time ? The problem is almost insoluble. And then there is Frogmore. The nineteenth-century sculpture in the royal mausoleum is reputed to be the most amazing of its amazing kind. I should like to see Frogmore. But the anniversary of Queen Victoria's death is the only day in the year when the temple is open to the public. The old queen died, I believe, in January. But what was the precise date ? And, if one enjoys the blessed liberty

to be elsewhere, how shall one reconcile oneself
to being in England at such a season? Frogmore, it seems, will have to remain unvisited.
And there are many other places, many other
dates and days, which, alas, I shall always miss.
I must even be resignedly content with the few
festivities whose times I can remember and
whose scene coincides, more or less, with that
of my existence in each particular portion of
the year.

One of these rare and solemn dates which I
happen never to forget is September the thirteenth. It is the feast of the Holy Face of
Lucca. And since Lucca is within thirty miles
of the seaside place where I spend the summer,
and since the middle of September is still
serenely and transparently summer by the
shores of the Mediterranean, the feast of the
Holy Face is counted among the captain jewels
of my year. At the religious function and the
ensuing fair I am, each September, a regular
attendant.

'By the Holy Face of Lucca!' It was
William the Conqueror's favourite oath. And
if I were in the habit of cursing and swearing,
I think it would also be mine. For it is a fine
oath, admirable both in form and substance.
'By the Holy Face of Lucca!' In whatever
language you pronounce them, the words reverberate, they rumble with the rumbling of genuine
poetry. And for any one who has ever seen

the Holy Face, how pregnant they are with power and magical compulsion ! For the Face, the Holy Face of Lucca, is certainly the strangest, the most impressive thing of its kind I have ever seen.

Imagine a huge wooden Christ, larger than life, not naked, as in later representations of the Crucifixion, but dressed in a long tunic, formally fluted with stiff Byzantine folds. The face is not the face of a dead, or dying, or even suffering man. It is the face of a man still violently alive, and the expression of its strong features is stern, is fierce, is even rather sinister. From the dark sockets of polished cedar wood two yellowish tawny eyes, made, apparently, of some precious stone, or perhaps of glass, stare out, slightly squinting, with an unsleeping balefulness. Such is the Holy Face. Tradition affirms it to be a true, contemporary portrait. History establishes the fact that it has been in Lucca for the best part of twelve hundred years. It is said that a rudderless and crewless ship miraculously brought it from Palestine to the beaches of Luni. The inhabitants of Sarzana claimed the sacred flotsam ; but the Holy Face did not wish to go to Sarzana. The oxen harnessed to the wagon in which it had been placed were divinely inspired to take the road to Lucca. And at Lucca the Face has remained ever since, working miracles, drawing crowds of pilgrims, protecting and at intervals failing to protect the city of its adoption from harm. Twice a year, at Easter time and on the thirteenth of September, the doors of its little domed tabernacle in the cathedral are thrown open, the candles are lighted, and the dark and formidable image, dressed up for the occasion in a jewelled overall and with a glittering crown on its head, stares down—with who knows what mysterious menace in its bright squinting eyes? —on the throng of its worshippers.

The official act of worship is a most handsome function. A little after sunset a procession of clergy forms up in the church of San Frediano. In the ancient darkness of the basilica a few candles light up the liturgical ballet. The stiff embroidered vestments, worn by generations of priests and from which the heads and hands of the present occupants emerge with an air of almost total irrelevance (for it is the sacramental carapace that matters; the little man who momentarily fills it is without significance), move hieratically hither and thither through the rich light and the velvet shadows. Under his baldaquin the jewelled old archbishop is a museum specimen. There is a forest of silvery mitres, spear-shaped against the darkness (bishops seem to be plentiful in Lucca). The choir boys wear lace and scarlet. There is a guard of halberdiers in a gaudily-pied mediæval uniform. The ritual charade is solemnly danced through. The procession emerges from the dark church into the twilight of the streets. The municipal band strikes up loud inappropriate music. We hurry off to the cathedral by a short cut to take our places for the function.

The Holy Face has always had a partiality for music. Yearly, through all these hundreds of years, it has been sung to and played at, it has been treated to symphonies, cantatas, solos on every instrument. During the eighteenth century the most celebrated *castrati* came from the ends of Italy to warble to it ; the most eminent professors of the violin, the flute, the oboe, the trombone scraped and blew before its shrine. Paganini himself, when he was living in Lucca in the court of Elisa Bonaparte, performed at the annual concerts in honour of the Face. Times have changed, and the image must now be content with local talent and a lower standard of musical excellence. True, the good will is always there ; the Lucchesi continue to do their musical best ; but their best is generally no more nor less than just dully creditable. Not always, however. I shall never forget what happened during my first visit to the Face. The musical programme that year was ambitious. There was to be a rendering, by choir and orchestra, of one of those vast oratorios which the clerical musician, Dom Perosi, composes in a strange and rather frightful mixture of the musical idioms of Palestrina, Wagner, and Verdi. The orchestra was enormous ; the choir was numbered by the hundred ; we waited in pleased anticipation for the music to begin. But when it did begin, what an astounding pandemonium ! Everybody played and sang like mad, but without apparently any reference to the playing and singing of anybody else. Of all the musical performances I have ever listened to it was the most Manchester-Liberal, the most Victorian-democratic. The conductor stood in the midst of them waving his arms ; but he was only a constitutional monarch —for show, not use. The performers had revolted against his despotism. Nor had they permitted themselves to be regimented into Prussian uniformity by any soul-destroying excess of rehearsal. Godwin's prophetic vision of a perfectly individualistic concert was here actually realized. The noise was hair-raising. But the performers were making it with so much gusto that, in the end, I was infected by their high spirits and enjoyed the hullabaloo almost as much as they did. That concert was symptomatic of the general anarchy of post-war Italy. Those times are now past. The Fascists have come, bringing order and discipline—even to the arts. When the Lucchesi play and sing to their Holy Face, they do it now with decorum, in a thoroughly professional and well-drilled manner. It is admirable, but dull. There are times, I must confess, when I regret the loud delirious blaring and bawling of the days of anarchy.

Almost more interesting than the official acts

of worship are the unofficial, the private and individual acts. I have spent hours in the cathedral watching the crowd before the shrine. The great church is full from morning till night. Men and women, young and old, they come in their thousands, from the town, from all the country round, to gaze on the authentic image of God. And the image is dark, threatening, and sinister. In the eyes of the worshippers I often detected a certain meditative disquiet. Not unnaturally. For if the face of Providence should really and in truth be like the Holy Face, why, then—then life is certainly no joke. Anxious to propitiate this rather appalling image of Destiny, the worshippers come pressing up to the shrine to deposit a little offering of silver or nickel and kiss the reliquary proffered to every almsgiver by the attendant priest. For two francs fifty perhaps Fate will be kind. But the Holy Face continues, unmoved, to squint inscrutable menace. Fixed by that sinister regard, and with the smell of incense in his nostrils, the darkness of the church around and above him, the most ordinary man begins to feel himself obscurely a Pascal. Metaphysical gulfs open before him. The mysteries of human destiny, of the future, of the purpose of life oppress and terrify his soul. The church is dark ; but in the midst of the darkness is a little island of candlelight. Oh, comfort ! But from the heart of the comforting light, incongruously jewelled, the dark face stares with squinting eyes, appalling, balefully mysterious.

But luckily, for those of us who are not Pascal, there is always a remedy. We can always turn our back on the Face, we can always leave the hollow darkness of the church. Outside, the sunlight pours down out of a flawless sky. The streets are full of people in their holiday best. At one of the gates of the city, in an open space beyond the walls, the merry-go-rounds are turning, the steam organs are playing the tunes that were popular four years ago on the other side of the Atlantic, the fat woman's drawers hang unmoving, like a huge forked pennon, in the windless air outside her booth. There is a crowd, a smell, an unceasing noise—music and shouting, roaring of circus lions, giggling of tickled girls, squealing from the switchback of deliciously frightened girls, laughing and whistling, tooting of cardboard trumpets, cracking of guns in the rifle-range, breaking of crockery, howling of babies, all blended together to form the huge and formless sound of human happiness. Pascal was wise, but wise too consciously, with too consistent a spirituality. For him the Holy Face was always present, haunting him with its dark menace, with the mystery of its baleful eyes. And if ever, in a moment of distraction, he forgot the metaphysical horror of the world and those abysses at his feet, it was with a pang of remorse that he came again to himself, to the self of spiritual consciousness. He thought it right to be haunted, he refused to enjoy the pleasures of the created world, he liked walking among the gulfs. In his excess of conscious wisdom he was mad ; for he sacrificed life to principles, to metaphysical abstractions, to the overmuch spirituality which is the negation of existence. He preferred death to life. Incomparably grosser and stupider than Pascal, almost immeasurably his inferiors, the men and women who move with shouting and laughter through the dusty heat of the fair are yet more wise than the philosopher. They are wise with the unconscious wisdom of the species, with the dumb, instinctive, physical wisdom of life itself. For it is life itself that, in the interests of living, commands them to be inconsistent. It is life itself that, having made them obscurely aware of Pascal's gulfs and horrors, bids them turn away from the baleful eyes of the Holy Face, bids them walk out of the dark, hushed, incense-smelling church into the sunlight, into the dust and whirling motion, the sweaty smell and the vast chaotic noise of the fair. It is life itself ; and I, for one, have more confidence in the rightness of life than in that of any individual man, even if the man be Pascal.

# REVOLUTIONS

'The Proletariat.' It was Karl Marx who enriched the dead and ugly gibbering of politicians and journalists and Thoughtful People (the gibbering which in certain circles is beautifully called ' the language of modern ideology ') with the word. ' The Proletariat.' For Marx those five syllables connoted something extremely unpleasant, something very discreditable to humanity at large and the bourgeoisie in particular. Pronouncing them, he thought of life in the English manufacturing towns in the first half of the nineteenth century. He thought of children working a two-hundred-and-sixteen-hour week for a shilling. Of women being used, instead of the more costly horse, in pulling trucks of coal along the galleries of mines. Of men performing endless tasks in filthy, degrading, and unwholesome surroundings in order to earn enough for themselves and their families just not to starve on. He thought of all the iniquitous things that had been done in the name of Progress and National Prosperity. Of all the atrocious wickedness which piously Christian ladies and gentlemen complacently accepted and even personally participated in, because they were supposed to be inevitable, like sunrise and sunset, because they were supposed to happen in accordance with the changeless, the positively divine, laws of Political Economy.

The wage-slaves of the early and middle nineteenth century were treated a good deal worse than most of the chattel slaves of antiquity and modern times. Naturally; for a chattel slave was a valuable possession, and nobody wantonly destroys valuable possessions. It was only when conquest had made slaves enormously plentiful and cheap that the owner class permitted itself to be extravagant with its labour resources. Thus, the Spaniards wiped out the whole of the aboriginal population of the West Indies in a few generations. The average life of an Indian slave in a mine was about a year. When he had been worked to death, the mine-owner bought another slave, for practically nothing. Slaves were a natural product of the soil, which the Spaniards felt themselves at liberty to waste, as the Americans now feel themselves at liberty to waste petroleum. But in normal times, when the supply of slaves was limited, owners were more careful of their possessions. The slave was then treated with at least as much consideration as a mule or a donkey. Nineteenth-century industrialists were in the position of conquerors having a suddenly dilated supply of slave labour on which to draw. Machinery had increased production, hitherto empty lands were supplying cheap food, while imported nitrates were increasing the home supply. It was therefore possible for the population to increase, and, when it is possible for the population to increase, it generally does increase, rapidly at first, and then, as a certain density is approached, with diminishing acceleration. The industrials of last century were living at the time of the population's most rapid increase. There was an endless supply of slaves. They could afford to be extravagant ; and, anaesthetizing their consciences with the consoling thought that it was all in accordance with those Iron Laws that were so popular in scientific circles at the period, and trusting with truly Christian faith that the wage-slaves would get their compensation in a Better World, they *were* extravagant—with a vengeance ! Wage-slaves were worked to death at high speed ; but there were always new ones coming in to take their places, fairly begging the capitalists to work *them* to death too. The efficiency of these slaves while being worked to death on starvation wages was, of course, very low ; but there were so many of them, and they cost so little, that the owners could rely on quantity to make up for any defect in quality.

Such was the position in the industrial world when Marx wrote his celebrated and almost universally unread work. The Proletariat, as he knew it, was exploited and victimized as only, in the slave-holding past, the conquered had been exploited and victimized. Marx's whole theory of contemporary history and future industrial development depended on the continual existence of precisely that particular Proletariat with which he was familiar. He did not foresee the possibility of that Proletariat ceasing to exist. For him it was to be for ever and inevitably victimized and exploited —that is, until revolution had founded the communist State.

The facts have proved him wrong. The Proletariat as he knew it had ceased—or, if that is too sweeping a statement, is ceasing —to exist in America and, to a less extent, industrialized Europe. The higher the degree of industrial development and material civilization (which is not at all the same thing, incidentally, as civilization *tout court*), the more complete has been the transformation of the Proletariat. In the most fully industrialized countries the Proletariat is no longer abject; it is prosperous, its way of life approximates to that of the bourgeoisie. No longer the victim, it is actually, in some places, coming to be the victimizer.

The causes of this change are many and diverse. In the depths of the human soul lies something which we rationalize as a demand for justice. It is an obscure perception of the necessity for balance in the affairs of life; we are conscious of it as a passion for equity, a hungering after righteousness. An obvious lack of balance in the outside world outrages this feeling for equity within us, gradually and cumulatively outrages it, until we are driven to react, often extravagantly, against the forces of disequilibrium. Just as the aristocratic power-holders of eighteenth-century France were driven, by their outraged sentiment of equity, to preach humanitarianism and equality, to give away their hereditary privileges and yield without a struggle to the demands of the revolutionaries, so the industrial-bourgeois power-holders of the nineteenth century passed laws to restrain their own cupidity, handed over more and more of their power to the Proletariat they had so outrageously oppressed, and even, in individual cases, took a strange masochistic pleasure in sacrificing themselves to the victims, serving the servants and being humiliated by the oppressed. If they had chosen to use their power ruthlessly, they could have gone on exploiting the wage-slaves as they exploited them in the earlier part of the century. But they simply could not make such a choice ; for the unbalanced world of the early industrial epoch was felt by the deepest self as an outrage. Hence, in the later nineteenth century, that 'craven fear of being great' which afflicted and still afflicts the class of masters. Here then is one cause of the change. It is a cause which historical materialists, who deal not with real human beings but with abstract

'Economic Men,' do not consider. It is none the less potent. In the world where historical materialists are at home, there were also good store of causes. Organization of the Proletariat. Revolutionary propaganda culminating in more or less revolutionary violence. And, above all, the momentous discovery that it pays the capitalist to have a prosperous Proletariat about him. It pays him to pay well, because those who are paid well buy well, particularly when hypnotized by the incessant suggestions of modern advertising. The policy of modern capitalism is to teach the Proletariat to be wasteful, to organize and facilitate its extravagance, and at the same time to make that extravagance possible by paying high wages in return for high production. The newly enriched Proletariat is suggested into spending what it earns, and even into mortgaging its future earnings in the purchase of objects which the advertisers persuasively affirm to be necessaries or at least indispensable luxuries. The money circulates and the prosperity of the modern industrial state is assured—until such time, at any rate, as the now extravagantly squandered resources of the planet begin to run low. But this eventuality is still, by the standards of an individual life, though not by those of history and infinitely less by those of geology, remote.

Meanwhile, what is happening, what is likely to happen in the future, to Karl Marx's Proletariat? Briefly, this is happening. It is becoming a branch of the bourgeoisie—a bourgeoisie that happens to work in factories and not in offices ; a bourgeoisie with oily instead of inky fingers. Out of working hours the way of life of these two branches of the modern bourgeoisie is the same. Inevitably, since they earn the same wages. In highly industrialized states, like America, there is a tendency towards equalization of income. There is a tendency for the unskilled workman to be paid as much as the skilled—or rather, since the machine tool is abolishing the difference between them, for skilled and unskilled to fuse into a single semi-skilled type with a given standard of wages— and for the manual worker to be paid as much as the professional man. (As things stand, he is often paid more than the professional. A constructional engineer overseeing the building of an American skyscraper may actually be paid less than a plasterer at work on the interior walls of the building. Bricklayers earn more than many doctors, draughtsmen, analytical chemists, teachers, and the like. This is partly due to the fact that the manual workers are more numerous and better organized than the brain workers and are in a better position to bargain with the capitalists ; partly to the overcrowding of the professions with the finished products of an educational system that turns out more would-be brain workers than there are places to fill—

or for that matter than there are brains to work !)
But to return to our transmogrified Proletariat.
The equalization of income—that happy consummation from which Mr. Bernard Shaw
expects all blessings automatically to flow—is in
process of being realized under the capitalist
system in America. What the immediate future
promises is a vast plateau of standardized income
—the plateau being composed of manual
labourers and the bulk of the class of clerks and
small professional men—with a relatively small
number of peaks rising from it to more or less
giddy heights of opulence. On these peaks will
be perched the hereditary owners of property,
the directors of industry and finance, and the
exceptionally able and successful professional
men. Given this transformation of the Proletariat into a branch of the bourgeoisie, given
this equalization—at an unprecedentedly high
level, and over an area unprecedentedly wide—
of standard income, the doctrines of socialism
lose most of their charm, and the communist
revolution becomes rather pointless. Those who
inhabit paradise do not dream of yet remoter
heavens (though it seems to me more than likely
that they yearn rather wistfully sometimes for
hell). The socialist paradise is a world where
all share equally, and the fulness of every man's
belly is guaranteed by the State. For the ordinary man the important items of this programme
will be the equality of sharing and the fulness of

the belly; he will not care who guarantees him these blessings, so long as guaranteed they are. If capitalism guarantees them, he will not dream of violently overthrowing capitalism for the sake of receiving precisely the same advantages from the socialist State. So that, if the present tendency continues, it would seem that the danger of a strictly communistic revolution in the highly developed industrial countries, like America, will disappear. What may happen, however, is a more gradual change in the present organization of capitalist society. A change for which capitalism itself will have been largely responsible. For by levelling up incomes at present low, in order that all may buy its productions, American capitalism is doing more for the democratization of society than any number of idealistic preachers of the Rights of Man. Indeed, it has transformed these famous rights and the claim that all men are equal from a polite fiction into the beginnings of a fact. In so doing, it seems to me, capitalism is preparing its own downfall—or rather the downfall of the extremely rich people who are now at the head of capitalist enterprise. For it is obvious that you cannot preach democracy, and not merely preach it, but actually give it practical realization throughout large tracts of society in terms of hard cash, without arousing in men the desire to be consistent and carry through the partial democratization of society to the end. We shall see, I believe, the realization of what seems at first sight a paradox—the imposition of complete democratic equality as the result, not of monstrous injustice, poverty, discontent, and consequent bloody revolution, but of partial equalization and universal prosperity. Past revolutions failed to produce the perfect democracy in whose name they were always made, because the great masses of the downtrodden were too abjectly poor to be able really to imagine the possibility of being the equals of their oppressors. Only those who were already well on the road towards economic equality with their masters ever profited by these revolutions. Revolutions always benefited the already prosperous and well organized. In America, under modern capitalism, the whole Proletariat is prosperous and well organized ; it is therefore in a position to feel its essential equality with its masters. It stands in the same relation with regard to the rich industrial overlords as did the English industrial and professional bourgeoisie with regard to the territorial magnates in 1832, or the lawyers, the merchants, the financiers, with regard to the French crown and its nobles in 1789. Incomes have been levelled up ; automatically there will arise a demand that they should also be levelled down. If a plasterer is worth as much as a constructional engineer, an oil-driller as much as a geologist (and according to modern capitalist-democratic theory they deserve the same wage inasmuch as each is a man or, in economic language, a consumer)—if this equality is considered just in theory and consecrated in practice by the payment of equal wages, then, it is obvious, there can be no justifiable inequality between the incomes of plasterer and engineer on the one hand, and company director and stockholder on the other. Either violently or, more probably, by a gradual and more or less painless process of propaganda, pressure of public opinion, and finally legislation, incomes will be levelled down as they are now being levelled up ; vast fortunes will be broken up ; ownership of joint-stock companies will be more and more widely distributed, and the directors of these enterprises will be paid as much as the most unskilled workman or the most learned scientific expert in their employ, as much and no more. For why should one consumer receive more than another ? No man has more than one belly to fill with food, one back to put clothes on to, one posterior to sit in a motor car with. A century should see the more or less complete realization, in the industrial West, of Mr. Shaw's dream of equal incomes for all.

And when the dream has been actualized, what then ? Will the spectre of revolution be definitively laid and humanity live happily ever afterwards ? Mr. Shaw, at any rate, seems to imagine so. Only once, if I remember, in the whole length of his *Guide to Socialism* does he even suggest that man does not live by equal incomes alone ; and then suggests it so slightly, so passingly, that the reader is still left with the impression that in equality of income lies the solution of every problem life has to offer. Fantastic doctrine, all the more absurd for being so apparently positivistic ! For nothing could be more chimerical than the notion that Man is the same thing as the Economic Man and that the problems of life, Man's life, can be solved by any merely economic arrangement. To suppose that the equalization of income could solve these problems is only slightly less absurd than to suppose that they could be solved by the universal installation of sanitary plumbing or the distribution of Ford cars to every member of the human species. That the equalization of income might in some ways be a good thing is obvious. (It might also, in others, be bad ; it would mean, for example, the complete practical realization of the democratic ideal, and this in its turn would mean, almost inevitably, the apotheosis of the lowest human values and the rule, spiritual and material, of the worst men.) But good or bad, the equalization of income can no more touch the real sources of present discontent than could any other large-scale book-keeping operation, such as, for example, a scheme to make possible the purchase of every conceivable commodity by deferred payments.

The real trouble with the present social and

industrial system is not that it makes some people very much richer than others, but that it makes life fundamentally unlivable for all. Now that not only work, but also leisure has been completely mechanized ; now that, with every fresh elaboration of the social organization, the individual finds himself yet further degraded from manhood towards the mere embodiment of a social function ; now that ready-made, creation-saving amusements are spreading an ever intenser boredom through ever wider spheres,—existence has become pointless and intolerable. Quite how pointless and how intolerable the great masses of materially-civilized humanity have not yet consciously realized. Only the more intelligent have consciously realized it as yet. To this realization the reaction of those whose intelligence is unaccompanied by some talent, some inner urge towards creation, is an intense hatred, a longing to destroy. This type of intelligent hater-of-everything has been admirably, and terrifyingly, portrayed by M. André Malraux in his novel, *Les Conquérants*. I recommend it to all sociologists.

The time is not far off when the whole population and not merely a few exceptionally intelligent individuals will consciously realize the fundamental unlivableness of life under the present régime. And what then ? Consult M. Malraux. The revolution that will then break out will not be communistic—there will be no need for such a revolution, as I have already shown, and besides nobody will believe in the betterment of humanity or in anything else whatever. It will be a nihilist revolution. Destruction for destruction's sake. Hate, universal hate, and an aimless and therefore complete and thorough smashing up of everything. And the levelling up of incomes, by accelerating the spread of universal mechanization (machinery is costly), will merely accelerate the coming of this great orgy of universal nihilism. The richer, the more materially civilized we become, the more speedily it will arrive. All that we can hope is that it will not come in our time.

# PASCAL

## I

### § 1. *The Orders*

'The infinite distance which separates bodies from minds symbolizes the infinitely more infinite distance between minds and charity; for charity is supernatural.

All bodies, the firmament, the stars, earth and its kingdoms, are not worth the least of minds: for the mind knows all these things and itself; and bodies, nothing.

All bodies together, and all minds together, and all their productions, are not worth the least movement of charity. That belongs to an infinitely higher order.

Roll all the bodies in the world into one and you will not be able to get one little thought out of them. That is impossible, it belongs to another order. Similarly, from all bodies and minds you cannot draw a movement of true charity; for that too is impossible, that too belongs to another order, or supernatural order.'

It would be easy to criticize these affirmations. To begin with, it is obvious that Pascal has no right to say that it is *impossible* for bodies to think. He is simply promoting his ignorance and his metaphysical prejudices to the rank of a general law. He would certainly have been less dogmatic if he had seen the highly emotional plants at the Bose Institute or Warburg's breathing carbon. True, it was not his fault that he lived before these experiments were made. But it *was* his fault that he did not see the purely philosophical objections to his analysis of reality. The idea of orders of existence is profound and fruitful, but only on condition that you choose your orders so that they correspond with observed reality. The Christian-Pascalian orders do not. Body, mind, and charity are not realities, but abstractions from reality. The solutions of continuity, so conspicuous in human life, are not between body, mind, and charity, but between different states of the total reality from which these hypothetical entities have been arbitrarily abstracted. Reality as we know it, is always a compound of the three elements into which Pascal divides it. And this in spite of idealism. For even if we grant the whole case of subjective idealism—and it is perhaps the only metaphysical system which is logically water-tight—we do nothing to diminish the importance of matter. Mind may be the creator of matter ; but that does not mean that it can deny the existence of its creature. The habit of seeing and touching material objects is a habit of which the mind cannot break itself. Matter may be illusory ; but it is a chronic illusion. Whether we like it or not, it is always there. So, for the benefit of the materialists, is mind. So are, intermittently, the psychological states which have been regarded, rightly or wrongly, as being states of contact with a higher spiritual world. For the purposes of classification we can divide the total reality into matter, mind, and, finally, charity, grace, the supernatural, God, or whatever other name you care to bestow on the third of the Pascalian orders. But we must beware of attributing actuality to these convenient abstractions ; we must resist the temptation to fall down and worship the intellectual images carved by ourselves out of the world (whether objective or subjective, it makes no difference) with which experience has made us familiar. True, the temptation is strong ; for the intellect has a special weakness for its own creations. Moreover, in this case the abstractions have actually been made the basis of a social reality. Men have actually tried to realize their classification in the structure of society. Pascal's mistake consists in applying to individual psychology and the world at large the hierarchical classification of social functions into mechanic and liberal, spiritual and lay. Indeed, he did more than merely apply it : he assumed that it was inherent in human nature itself and even in non-human nature —that the caste system had an objective existence in the universe. A convenient social arrangement was thus promoted by him to the rank of a primordial fact of human psychology and cosmic structure. True, the particular social arrangement in question was a very convenient one. All the great qualitative civilizations have been hierarchical. The fine arts and the arts of life have flourished most luxuriantly in those societies, in which a very sharp distinction was drawn between mechanic and liberal occupations. Our modern civilization is quantitative and democratic. We draw no distinctions between mechanic and liberal— only between rich and poor. Western society has been wholly laicized—with most depressing effects on those human activities hitherto regarded as the most valuable. America has twenty-five million motor cars, but almost no original art.

Pascal took the social hierarchy for granted. Naturally. He had never heard of a society in which the distinction between the lay and the spiritual was not sharply drawn. But he was not for that reason justified in supposing that the hierarchy existed objectively in nature.

Reality, as we know it, is an organic whole. Separable in theory, the three Pascalian orders are in fact indissolubly wedded. Nor must we forget that matter, mind, and the supernatural are arbitrary abstractions from experience, and that other systems of classification are easily conceivable. The observed solutions of continuity are not, as Pascal maintains, between

the three abstractions, which have no existence
outside the classifying intellect.  They are rather
between different states of the total reality as
experienced by different individuals, and by the
same individual at different times.  Between
the sick man and the healthy man, between the
hungry and the full, the lustful and the satiated,
the young and the old, between the normally
and abnormally gifted, between the cultured
European and the primitive Papuan, there yawn
great gulfs of separation.

Those who would learn how far it is possible
for some one with an unusual temperament to
dissociate himself from the moral and intellectual
reality accepted as normal by the majority of
Europeans should read Dostoievsky's *Notes from
Underground*.  And what profoundly dissimilar
universes may be inhabited by the same man
at different seasons !  In the terrifying *Death of
Ivan Ilyitch* Tolstoy has shown how deep, how wide,
is the gulf which separates a man in health from
the 'same man' when death has laid its hand
upon him.  These two works of fiction are worth
a whole library of treatises on the theory of
knowledge and the nature of reality.  Most
philosophical argument is argument at cross
purposes ; it is the angry shouting at one another
of two people who use the same words but mean
different things by them.  It is the hopeless and
futile squabbling of beings who belong in taste
and feeling to distinct zoological species.  One

philosopher abuses another for having stupid and wicked views about the nature of things, without realizing that the things about whose nature he has such decided opinions are entirely different from the things the other fellow has been discussing. Their universes are parallel to one another ; this side of infinity they do not meet.

## § 2. *Private Universes*

Now, the universe in which each individual lives is an affair partly of heredity, partly of acquired habit. A man may be born with a strong tendency to inhabit one kind of universe rather than another ; but this congenital tendency is never completely exclusive. The cosmos in which each of us lives is at least as much a product of education as of physiological inheritance ; habit and a lifetime of repetitions determine its form and content. Its boundaries are fixed conventionally by a kind of inward Treaty of Versailles. It is a treaty, however, which Nature refuses to be rigidly and permanently bound by. When it suits the natural, hereditary man to recognize the Soviets of his own spirit, to make war on one of his Glorious Allies, or disestablish his private Church, he does so, with or without compunction, until the illegal action produces in due course a reaction towards legality, and he feels himself compelled once more to ratify his treaty. Men feel bound by a kind of intellectual and moral patriotism to defend in theory (even though in act they may betray it) the particular cosmos of their choice ; they are jingo positivists, chauvinistically mystical. But if they were sincere with themselves they would realize that these patriotic ardours in matters of philosophy are not merely misplaced, but without justification. No man is by nature exclusively domiciled in one universe  All lives—even the lives of the men and women who have the most strongly - marked congenital tendencies — are passed under at least two flags and generally under many more. Even the most ardent positivist is sometimes carried away by a wave of mystical emotion. Even the most frenzied absolute-hunters, aesthetes, and idealists must compromise with the gross world of relativity and practice to the extent of eating, taking shelter from the weather, behaving at least conventionally enough to keep out of the clutches of the police. Even Podsnap may once have had inklings of the nature of love and poetry. Even the healthiest man, the most bottomlessly ' average ' and hard-headed of Ivan Ilyitches, feels the approach of death at least once in the course of his existence. Even the most pious Catholic is sometimes a Pyrrhonist—nay, *ought* to be a Pyrrhonist (it is Pascal himself who says it). The only completely consistent people are the dead ; the living are never anything but

233

diverse. But such is man's pride, such his intellectually vicious love of system and fixity, such his terror and hatred of life, that the majority of human beings refuse to accept the facts. Men do not want to admit that they are what in fact they are—each one a colony of separate individuals, of whom now one and now another consciously lives with the life that animates the whole organism and directs its destinies. They want, in their pride and their terror, to be monsters of stiff consistency ; they pretend, in the teeth of the facts, that they are one person all the time, thinking one set of thoughts, pursuing one course of action throughout life. They insist on being *either* Pascal *or* Voltaire, *either* Podsnap *or* Keats, when in fact they are potentially always, and at different times actually, a little of what each of these personages symbolically stands for and a great deal more beside. My music, like that of every other living and conscious being, is a counterpoint, not a single melody, a succession of harmonies and discords. I am now one person and now another, ' aussi différent de moi-même,' in La Rochefoucauld's words, ' que des autres.' And I am always potentially and sometimes actually and consciously both at once. In spite or rather because of this (for every 'in spite' is really a 'because') I have tried to pretend that I was superhumanly consistent, I have tried to force myself to be an embodiment of a principle, a walking system.

But one can only become consistent by becoming petrified ; and a rigid philosophical system is only possible on condition that one refuses to consider all those necessarily numerous aspects of reality which do not permit themselves to be explained in terms of it. For me, the pleasures of living and understanding have come to outweigh the pleasures, the very real pleasures (for the consciousness of being a man of principle and system is extremely satisfying to the vanity), of pretending to be consistent. I prefer to be dangerously free and alive to being safely mummified. Therefore I indulge my inconsistencies. I try to be sincerely myself—that is to say, I try to be sincerely all the numerous people who live inside my skin and take their turn at being the master of my fate.

It is, then, as a mixed being, as a colony of free and living minds, not as a single mind irrevocably committed, like a fossil fly in amber, to a single system of ideas, that I now propose to write of Pascal. As a positivist first of all, for the rationalizing part is one I find only too easy to play. More sympathetically next, in the guise of a Pascalian ; for I too have sometimes found myself in other worlds than those familiar to the positivist, I too have chased the absolute in those remote strange regions beyond the borders of the quotidian consciousness. And finally as a worshipper of life, who accepts all the conflicting facts of human existence and tries to frame a way of life and a philosophy (a necessarily inconsistent way, a realistically self-contradictory philosophy) in accordance with them. To make a map of a mountain, to fix its position in space, we must look at it from every side, we must go all round it, climb all over it. It is the same with a man as with a mountain. A single observation does not suffice to fix his form and define his position in relation to the rest of the world ; he must be looked at from all sides. This is what I have tried to do with Pascal. There is little biography in this essay and no circumambient history. (To those who would see Pascal in relation to his own century I would recommend such works as Strowski's *Pascal et son Temps* and Chevalier's *Pascal*.) I have sought to situate him in the eternal landscape of human psychology, to fix his position in relation to its unchanging features—to the body, the instincts, the passions and feelings, the speculative mind. Indeed, to any one who takes the trouble to read this study it will be sufficiently apparent that its subject is not really Pascal at all, but this psychological landscape. Pascal is really only an excuse and a convenience. If I choose to write about him it is because he raises, either by implication in his life, or explicitly in his writings, practically all the major problems of philosophy and conduct. And raises them how masterfully ! Never has the case against life been put with such subtlety, such elegance, such persuasive cogency, such admirable succintness. He explored the same country as I am now exploring ; went, saw, and found it detestable. He said so, exhaustively—for his quick eyes saw everything. All that, from his side, could be said, he said. His reports have accompanied me on my psychological travels ; they have been my Baedeker. I have compared his descriptions with the originals, his comments with my own reactions. In the margin of the guide-book I have pencilled a few reflections. This essay is made up of them. Pascal is only incidentally its subject.

## § 3. *The Riddle*

In the form in which men have posed it, the Riddle of the Universe requires a theological answer. Suffering and enjoying, men want to know why they enjoy and to what end they suffer. They see good things and evil things, beautiful things and ugly, and they want to find a reason—a final and absolute reason —why these things should be as they are. It is extremely significant, however, that it is only in regard to matters which touch them very closely that men look for theological reasons —and not only look, but find as well, and in what quantities ! With regard to matters which do not touch them to the quick, matters which are, so to speak, at a certain psychological distance from themselves, they are relatively incurious. They make no effort to find a theological explanation for them ; they see the absurdity, the hopelessness, of even looking for such an explanation. What, for example, is the final, the theological reason for grass being green and sunflowers yellow? One has only to put the question to perceive that it is quite unanswerable. We can talk about light-waves, vibrating electrons, chlorophyll molecules, and such like ; but any explanation we may offer in terms of these entities will only be an explanation of *how* grass is green, not of *why* it is green. There is no ' why '—none, at any rate, that we can conceivably discover. Grass is green because that is how we see it ; in other words, it's green because it *is* green. Now, there is no difference in kind between a green fact and a painful or beautiful fact, between a fact that is the colour of sunflowers and facts that are good or hellish : one class of facts is psychologically more remote than the other, that is all. Things are noble or agonizing because they are so. Any attempt to explain why they should be so is as inevitably predestined to failure as the attempt to explain why grass is green. In regard to greenness and other psychologically distant phenomena men have recognized the hopelessness of the task and no longer try to propound theological explanations. But they still continue to rack their brains over the riddles of the moral and aesthetic universes, they go on inventing answers and even believing in them.

## § 4. *Answers to the Riddle*

Pascal was well acquainted with the psychological reasons for the asking and answering of cosmic riddles. ' Il est bon,' he says, ' d'être lassé et fatigué par l'inutile recherche du vrai bien, afin de tendre les bras au Libérateur.' Borrowing a phrase from the Psalmist, he returns in another passage to the same theme. ' The waters of Babylon flow and fall and sweep away. O holy Zion, where all is stable and where nothing falls ! ' The words are Pascal's, but they express an ancient and almost universal yearning, the yearning that has given birth to all the Gods and Goods, all the Truths and Beauties, all the Justices, the Revelations, the Ones, the Rights of a bewildered and suffering humanity. For the Absolute has all too human parents. Fatigue and perplexity, wretchedness and the sentiment of transience, the longing for certainty, the desire for moral justification— these are its ancestors. ' Change and decay,' writes the author of the most popular of English hymns, ' change and decay in all around I see ; O Thou who changest not, abide with me.' From the fact of change and decay the logic of desire deduces the existence of something

changeless. Appearances are multiple and
chaotic ; if only things were simpler, easier to
understand ! The wish creates ; it is desirable
that there should be noumena ; therefore noumena exist and the noumenal world is more
truly real than the world of everyday life. *Quod
erat demonstrandum.* A similar conjuring trick
produces the One out of the deplorably puzzling
Many, draws the Good and the Beautiful out
of the seething hotch-potch of diverse human
tastes and sensibilities and interests, deduces
Justice from our actual inequalities, and absolute
Truth from the necessary and unescapable relativities of daily life. It is by an exactly similar
process that children invent imaginary play-
mates to amuse their solitudes and transform
a dull, uninteresting piece of wood into a horse,
a ship, a railway train—what you will. The
difference between children and grown-ups is
that children do not try to justify their compensatory imaginations intellectually ; whereas
grown-ups, or rather adolescents (for the vast
majority of chronological adults have never
grown, if they have emerged from childhood
at all, beyond adolescence), do make the attempt.
The newly conscious and the newly rational
have all the defects of the newly rich ; they
make a vulgar parade of their possessions, they
swaggeringly advertise their powers. They re-
view all the biologically useful beliefs, all the
life-stimulating fancies of individual or racial

childhood, and pretentiously 'explain' them in terms of newly-discovered rationalism. The gods and fairies are replaced by abstract noumena. Zeus fades away into Justice, Power, Oneness ; Athene becomes Wisdom ; Aphrodite degenerates into Intellectual Beauty. In recent times this replacement of the old deities by hypostasized abstractions has been called 'modernism,' and regarded, quaintly enough, as a spiritual advance, a liberation, a progress towards Truth. In reality, of course, the noumena invented by adolescent minds are, absolutely speaking, as false (or as true, there is no means of discovering which) as the mythological personages whose place they have usurped. As vital symbols they are much less adequate. The childish fancies are inspired directly by life. The adolescent noumena are abstractions from life, flights from diversity into disembodied oneness. The noumenal world is a most inadequate substitute for fairyland and Olympus.

## § 5. *Pascal and Rationalism*

Pascal was an intellectual adult who deliberately forced himself to think like a Christian philosopher—that is to say, like an unstably-balanced compound of child and adolescent. Towards the complacencies of the full-blown adolescent he was ruthless. A critic so acute, so intellectually grown-up, could not be expected to swallow the pseudo-logical arguments of the rationalists. 'Laugh at philosophy,' was his advice, 'and you are a true philosopher.' He himself mocked wittily. 'Feu M. Pascal,' wrote a contemporary, 'appelait la philosophie cartésienne le *Roman de la Nature*, semblable à Don Quichotte.' What a high and, to my mind, what an undeserved compliment to Descartes! Most of those curious romances which we call philosophical systems are more like Sidney's *Arcadia* or the *Grand Cyrus* than *Don Quixote*. How proud I should be, if I were a metaphysician, to be mentioned in the same breath with Cervantes! But Descartes, if he had heard the sally, would certainly have been more pained by it than pleased. For Descartes was a rationalist; he believed in the reality of his abstractions. Inventing fictions, he imagined that he was revealing the Truth. Pascal knew better. Pascal was a critic and a realist; Pascal was intellectually grown-up. 'Our soul,' he said, 'is thrown into the body, where it finds matter, time, dimension. Thereon it reasons and calls that nature and necessity, and cannot believe in anything else.' And again: 'It is not in our capacity to know what God is, nor whether He exists.' We might be reading a discourse, mercifully abbreviated, by Kant. It is unnecessary for me to rehearse the arguments by means of which Pascal demolished the pretensions of the rationalists to attain by human means to the knowledge of any absolute whatever. Montaigne's armoury was conveniently at hand ; he sharpened and envenomed the Pyrrhonian weapons with which it was stored. Elegantly, artistically, but without mercy, the rationalists were slaughtered. Rather more than a hundred years later they were slaughtered again by Kant, and, after the passage of another century, yet once more, and this time with a Tamburlane-like ferocity and thoroughness, by Nietzsche. Pragmatists, humanists, philosophers of science continue the massacre. Hewn down, the rationalists sprout again like the Hydra's heads. The learned and the unlearned world is crammed with them. This survival of rationalism in the teeth of an unescapable destructive criticism is a tribute, if not to humanity's intelligence, at least to its love of life. For rationalism, in its rather ponderous and silly way, is an illusion with a biological value, a vital lie. 'When the truth of a thing is unknown,' said Pascal, two hundred years before Nietzsche, 'it is good that there should be a common error to fix men's minds.' The only defect of rationalism as a vital lie is that it is insufficiently vital. Vital lie for vital lie, polytheistic mythology is preferable to the rationalists' system of abstractions. The falsehood of rationalism is manifest to any one who is ready to examine its paralogisms with the

eyes of unprejudiced and dispassionate intelligence. If it stimulates life, it does so only
feebly. Being in the most eminent degree intelligent, Pascal realized that there was no hope
of attaining by rational means the absolutes
for which he longed. A rational absolute is
a contradiction in terms. The only absolute
which a man of intelligence can believe in is
an irrational one. It was his realization of
the stupidity of rationalism that confirmed
Pascal in his catholicism.

## § 6. *Revelation*

' C'est en manquant de preuves,' he says of
the Christians, ' qu'ils ne manquent pas de sens.'
The rationalists who are never in want of proofs
thereby prove their own want of intelligence.
Where absolutes are concerned, reason is unreasonable. ' Il n'y a rien si conforme à la raison
que ce désaveu de la raison.' Being reasonable,
Pascal disavowed rationalism and attached himself to revelation. The absolutes of revelation
must be genuine absolutes, firm, eternal in the
midst of life's indefinite flux, untainted with
contingency. They *must* be genuine, because
revelation is, by definition, non-human. But
the definition of non-humanity is itself human ;
and the revelations are couched in human language, and are the work of individual human
beings who lived all too humanly in space and

time. We are fatally back again among the relativities. Nor will all the ingenious historical arguments contained in the later sections of the *Pensées* (arguments which Cardinal Newman was later to develop with his usual subtlety) do anything to get us out of the relativities. Pascal tried to demonstrate the Historical Truth of the Christian revelation. But, alas! there is no such thing as Historical Truth—there are only more or less probable opinions about the past, opinions which change from generation to generation. History is a function, mathematically speaking, of the degree of ignorance and of the personal prejudices of historians. The history of an epoch which has left very few documents is at the mercy of archæological research; a happy discovery may necessitate its radical revision from one day to the next. In cases where circumstances seem to have condemned us to a definitive and permanent ignorance, we might expect historical opinions to be at least as settled as the historians' lack of knowledge. But this occurs only when the events in question are indifferent. So long as past events continue to possess a certain actuality their history will vary from age to age, and the same documents will be reinterpreted, the same definitive ignorance will be made the basis of ever new opinions. Where documents are numerous and contradictory (and such is the fallibility of human testimony that numerous documents are always contradictory), each his-

torian will select the evidence which fits in with
his own prejudices, and ignore or disparage all
the rest. The nearest approach to Historical
Truth is the fixed opinion entertained by suc-
cessive historians about past events in which they
take no vital interest. Opinions about mediæval land tenure are not likely to undergo serious
fluctuations, for the good reason that the question
of mediæval land tenure possesses, and will
doubtless continue to possess, a purely academic
interest. Christianity, on the other hand, is not
an academic question. The documents dealing
with the origins of the religion are therefore
certain to undergo a constant process of rein-
terpretation. Doubtful human testimonies (all
human testimony is doubtful) have given birth
to, and will continue, so long as Christianity preserves a more than academic interest, to justify,
a variety of opinions in variously constituted,
variously prejudiced minds. This is the reality
out of which Pascal tried to extract that non-
existent thing, the Historical Truth.


## § 7. *Historical Grounds of Pascal's Faith*

It may seem strange that Pascal should not
have realized the uselessness of trying to find an
absolute even in revealed religion. But if he
failed to treat catholicism as realistically as he
treated other doctrines, that was because he
wanted to believe in its absolutes. He felt a need

for absolutes, and this temperamental need was stronger than his intelligence. Of Pascal's temperament, of that strange soul of his, ' naturaliter Christiana,' but with such a special and rather dreadful kind of Christianity, I shall speak later. In this place I shall only mention the external circumstances which quickened his desire to believe in the Catholic absolutes. Those middle years of the seventeenth century, which were the historical scene of Pascal's brief existence, were years, for Europe, of more than ordinary restlessness and misery. Germany was being devastated by the most bloodthirsty of religious wars. In England the Parliament was fighting with the King. France was agitated by the pointless skirmishing of the Fronde. It was the Europe, in a word, of Callot's etchings. Along its roads marched companies of hungry and marauding pikemen ; its crows were busy on the carcases that dangled from the branches of every wellgrown oak. There was raping and casual plundering, shooting and hanging in plenty, with torture to relieve the monotony and breakings on the wheel as a Sunday treat. To Pascal, as he looked at the world about him, peace seemed the supremely desirable thing, peace and order. The political situation was much the same as that which, in our own days, made Mussolini the saviour of his country, justified Primo de Rivera, and recruited so many adherents to the cause of the Action Française. Our modern anarchy has made of the unbelieving Charles Maurras an enthusiastic upholder of Catholicism. Pascal was a Maurras who believed in Catholicism to the point of thinking it true as well as politically useful, of regarding it as being good for himself as well as for the lower classes. Pascal's remedy for the disorders of his time was simple : passive obedience to the legally constituted authority—to the King in France, for example, to the Republic in Venice. For men to rebel against the masters Providence has given them is a sin ; the worst of evils is civil war. It is the political wisdom of despair. To long, in the midst of anarchy, for peace and order at any price one need not be a Christian. Pascal's counsels of passive despair took their origin in political events, not in his Catholic convictions. But his Catholic convictions justified them. For man, being utterly corrupt, is incapable of bringing forth, without divine assistance, any good thing. It is therefore folly to rebel, folly to wish to change existing institutions ; for the new state of things, being the work of corrupted human nature, must infallibly be as bad as that which it replaces. The wise man is therefore he who accepts the existing order, not because it is just or makes men happy, but simply because it exists and because no other order would be any juster or succeed in making men any happier.

History shows that there is a good deal of truth

in Pascal's views. The hopes of revolutionaries have always been disappointed. But for any one who values life as life, this is no argument against attempting revolutions. The faith in the efficacy of revolutions (however ill-founded events may prove it to be) is a stimulus to present living, a spur to present action and thought. In the attempt to realize the illusory aims of revolution, men are induced to live more intensely in the present, to think, do, and suffer with a heightened energy ; the result of this is that they create a new reality (very different, no doubt, from that which they had hoped to create, but that does not matter ; the important fact is that it is new). The new reality imposes new hopes and faiths on those who live in the midst of it, and the new hopes and faiths stimulate men to intenser living and the creation of yet another new reality. And so on indefinitely. But this is an argument which would most certainly have failed to make Pascal a revolutionary. Pascal had no wish to have present living intensified. He detested present living. For present living is a tissue of concupiscences, and therefore thoroughly anti-Christian. He would have liked to see present living abolished ; therefore he had no patience with any doctrine, religious, philosophical, or social, calculated to enhance the vital process. The Christianity which he chose to practise and believe in was duly anti-vital.

## § 8. *Personal Grounds : the Ecstasy*

It is, I repeat, in Callot's etchings of the Horrors of War that the political reasons for Pascal's Catholicism are to be found, just as it is in the newspaper man's snapshots of proletarian mobs 'demonstrating' in the industrial towns and capitalist mobs drearily and expensively amusing themselves at Monte Carlo, that we must look for an explanation of the Catholicism of M. Maurras. But Pascal had other, more cogent, personal reasons for believing. The record of his sudden apocalyptic conversion—that famous 'Memorial' which was found, after his death, sewn like a talisman in the lining of his clothes— is a document of the highest interest, not only for the light it throws on Pascal himself, but also for what it tells us of the mystical experience in general and of the way in which that experience is interpreted. I reproduce the text in its entirety :—

L'an de grace 1654.
Lundy 23 novembre, jour de St. Clement, pape
et martir et autres au martirologe
veille de St. Chrysogone martir, et autres
Depuis environ dix heures et demy du soir jusques environ
minuit et demy.

Feu

Dieu d'Abraham, Dieu d'Isaac, Dieu de Jacob
Non des philosophes et des sçavans
Certitude, certitude sentiment Joye Paix.

250

Dieu de Jesus Christ
Deum meum et Deum vestrum
Ton Dieu sera mon Dieu
Oubly du monde et de tout, hormis Dieu.
ne se trouve que par les voyes enseignées dans l'Evangile
Grandeur de l'ame humaine
Père juste, le monde ne t'a point connu, mais je t'ay connu
Joye, joye, joye, pleurs de joye
Je m'en suis separé
Dereliquerunt me fontem aquae vivae
Mon Dieu, me quitterez-vous ?
Que je n'en sois pas separé éternellement
Je m'en suis separé ; je l'ay fui renoncé crucifié
Que je n'en sois jamais separé
ne se conserve que par les voyes enseignées dans l'Evangile
Renonciation totalle et douce.
Soumission totale à Jesus Christ et mon directeur
Eternellement en joye pour un jour d'exercice sur la terre.
Non obliviscar sermones tuas. Amen.

To any one who reads this 'Memorial' with
care it is at once obvious that its substance is
not homogeneous. It is, so to speak, stratified,
built up of alternate layers of direct experience
and intellectual interpretations after the fact.
Even the date is a mixture of straightforward
chronology and Christian hagiography. Monday, November the twenty-third, is also the eve
of St. Chrysogonus's day. With the first word,
'feu,' we are in the midst of pure experience.
Fire—it is the mystical rapture in the raw, so to
speak, and undigested. The next two lines are
layers of interpretation. Meditating on that

inward conflagration which burns in the ' feu '
of the first line, Pascal comes to the conclusion
that it has been lighted by 'the God of Abraham,
Isaac, and Jacob, not of the philosophers and
men of science.' There follows another stratum
of pure experience. ' Certitude, certitude, feeling, joy, peace ' ; the violence of rapture has
been succeeded by ecstatic calm. The mind
once more steps in and explains these experiences
in terms of a hypothesis which Pascal has tele-
graphically summarized in the words ' Dieu de
Jésus Christ.'

With ' Oubly du monde et de toute, hormis
Dieu ' we move away from the realm of interpretation towards that of immediate psychological
experience. Proceeding, we pass through several
strata of doctrinal Meditations, to reach in 'Joye,
joye, joye, pleurs de joye ' yet another layer of
pure experience. The next lines, from ' Je m'en
suis separé' to ' Que je n'en sois pas separé éternellement,' are strata of mixed substance—
records of direct or remembered experiences
conditioned, as to mode and quality, by a theological hypothesis. For, it is obvious, emotional
experience and intellectual interpretation of that
experience cannot be kept permanently separated
in alternating strata. Crudely and schematic-
ally, what happens is this : something is directly
experienced ; this experience is intellectually
interpreted, generally in terms of some existing
system of metaphysics or mythology ; the myth,

the philosophical system are regarded as true and become in their turn the source of new experiences and the channels through which the old emotions must pass. Pascal's ' Memorial ' illustrates the whole process. In what I may call its upper strata we have alternating layers of pure experience and pure interpretation—fire and the God of Abraham ; Certitude, Joy, Peace, and the God of Jesus Christ. Later on he gives expression to what I may call secondary emotions—emotions aroused in him by his reflections on the after-the-fact interpretation of the primary mystical emotions. He feels the terror of being separated from the God he has called in to explain his original sensations of joy and peace.

That the mystical experience need not necessarily be interpreted as Pascal interpreted it, is obvious. Substantially similar experiences have been explained in terms of Buddhism, Brahmanism, Mohammedanism, Taoism, Shamanism, Neo-Platonism, and countless other religions and philosophies. They have also frequently been left uninterpreted. In the correspondence of William James, for example, there is an interesting letter describing what is obviously a full-blown ecstasy, for which, however, James does not presume to suggest any metaphysical explanation. Wisely ; for the mystical experience is like all other primary psychological facts, susceptible of none but a tautological explanation.

These things happen because they do happen, because that is what the human mind happens to be like. Between the various explanatory hypotheses in terms of the 'God of Abraham,' Nirvana, Allah, and the rest, there is nothing to choose ; in so far as each of them claims to be the unattainable Truth, and all of them postulate a knowledge of the unknowable Absolute, they are all equally ill-founded.

### § 9. *The Humanist and the Christian*

Pascal's metaphysic may be described as a kind of positivistic Pyrrhonism tempered, and indeed flatly denied, by dogmatic Christianity. His morality is similarly self-contradictory. For Pascal prescribes at the same time a more than Aristotelian moderation and a Christian excess. He rebukes men for pretentiously trying to be angels, and in the same breath rebukes them for being human. 'L'homme est ni ange ni bête, et le malheur veut que qui veut faire l'ange fait la bête.' Alas ! the facts prove Pascal only too right. The would-be angels of this world 'font la bête' in every possible sense of the word : they become either beasts or silly—frequently both at once. The realistic wisdom of Pascal reveals itself in a remark like the following : 'I am perfectly willing to take my place in it [the middle, human world between beast and angel], and refuse to be at the lower end, not because it is low, but because it is an end ; for I should equally refuse to be placed at the upper extremity.' And again : ' To step out of the middle way is to step out of humanity. The greatness of the human soul consists in knowing how to hold to the middle way.' Pascal lets fall many other aphorisms of the same kind. ' It is not good to be too free. It is not good to have all the necessities of life.' ' Les grands efforts de l'esprit, où l'âme touche quelquefois, sont choses où elle ne se tient pas ; elle y saute quelquefois.' ' How much a man's virtue is capable of must be measured, not by his efforts, but by his ordinary behaviour.' And so on.

But this humanistic wisdom was, in Pascal, only occasional and theoretical. He himself did not practise what he preached. What he practised is admiringly recorded in his sister's biography. ' Always and in all things he used to act on principles. . . . It was not possible for him to abstain from using his senses ; but when necessity obliged him to give them some pleasure he had a wonderful capacity for averting his spirit so that it should take no part in the pleasure. At meals we never heard him praise the viands that were served him. . . . And when anybody . . . admired the excellence of some dish, he could not abide it ; for he called that " being sensual " . . . because, said he, it was a sign that one ate to please one's taste, a thing that was always wrong. . . . In the early days of his retreat he had calculated the amount of food required for the needs of his stomach, and from that time forward, whatever might be his appetite, he never passed that measure ; and whatever disgust he might feel, he made a point of eating the quantity he had fixed.' His stomach was not the only part of him that Pascal mortified. ' The spirit of mortification, which is the very spirit of charity,' inspired him to have a spiked iron belt made for himself. This belt he would put on whenever a visitor came to see him, and when he found himself taking pleasure in the conversation, or feeling in the least vain of his powers as a spiritual guide, ' Il se donnait des coups de coude pour redoubler la violence des piqûres, et se faire ensuite ressouvenir de son devoir.' Later, when his illness made it impossible for him to concentrate on his studies, he wore the belt continually, that the pricking of it might excite his mind to continual fervour.

In the intervals of these ascetic practices Pascal wrote on the necessity of keeping to the middle road, of remaining human. But this was all abstraction and theory. Christianity would not permit him to behave hellenically, just as it would not permit him to think like a Pyrrhonist. Pascal, the philosopher, looked at the world and concluded that ' qui veut faire l'ange fait la bête.' But revealed religion insisted that he should try to be an angel of self-denial, of conscious and consistent other-worldliness. He made the effort and became—what? Perhaps an angel in some other world; who knows? The philosopher can only answer for this; and in this world the would-be angel duly and punctually 'faisait la bête.' That he had a horror of every form of sensuality goes without saying. He hated all lovers and their desires. He hated the beauty that inspired these impure longings. 'If I happened to say, for example, that I had seen a handsome woman,' writes Mme. Périer, 'he would reprimand me, saying that such a remark should never be made in the presence of servants and young people, as I did not know what thoughts it might excite in them.' Of marriage he said, in a letter to his sister, that it was 'une espèce d'homicide et comme un déicide.' For those who marry become exclusively interested in the creature, not the creator; the man who loves a woman kills God in his own mind and, by killing God, in the end kills himself—eternally.

He mistrusted even maternal love. 'Je n'oserais dire,' writes Mme. Périer, 'qu'il ne pouvait même souffrir les caresses que je recevais de mes enfants; il prétendait que cela ne pouvait que leur nuire, qu'on leur pouvait témoigner de la tendresse en mille autres manières.' Towards the end of his life this man of principles would not even permit himself the pleasure of being attached to his friends and relations, nor of being loved by them in return. 'It was one of the fundamental maxims of his piety never to allow any one to love him with attachment ; and he gave it to be understood that this was a fault in regard to which men did not examine themselves with sufficient care, a fault that had serious consequences, and the more to be feared in that it often seemed to us devoid of all danger.' How dangerous Pascal himself considered it, may be judged from these words from a little memorandum which he carried about with him, and which was found on his person after his death : 'That people should attach themselves to me is not just. . . . I should be deceiving those in whom I inspired the wish to do so ; for I am no man's goal and have nothing wherewith to satisfy them. . . . If I make people love me, if I attract them to myself, I am guilty ; for their lives and all their cares should be devoted to attaching themselves to God or to seeking him.'

§ 10. *The Sick Ascetic*

Principles, the desire to be angelically consistent, caused him to ' faire la bête ' outside the sphere of personal behaviour and human relations as well as within. Art, for example, he disliked because it was different from morality, and it was to morality that he had given his exclusive allegiance. In art, he says, ' la règle est [he means ' doit être '] l'honnêteté. Poète et non honnête homme.' How he hated the poets for having other rules than those of virtue and for behaving like men rather than like good men ! He felt all the Puritan's disapproval of the theatre because it made people think about love, and because it gave them pleasure. Anything that gave pleasure was odious to this great hater. That section of the *Pensées* which deals with worldly distractions is perhaps the most vigorous of the whole book ; hatred improved his style. He loathed his fellows for being able to amuse themselves. He would have liked all men to be as he himself was—racked with incessant pain, sleepless, exhausted by illness. ' Sickness,' he affirmed, ' is the Christian's natural state ; for in sickness a man is as he ought always to be—in a state, that is to say, of suffering, of pain, of privation from all the pleasures of the senses, exempt from all passions.' Such was the opinion of Pascal, the Christian dogmatist ; Pascal, the philosopher, looked at the matter rather differently. ' We have another principle of error in our illnesses. They spoil our judgment and sense.' The Christian's natural state is therefore, philosophically, a state of chronic error. The sick man has no right to pass judgment on the activities of health. A man who has no ear is not the best critic of Mozart's quartets ; and similarly a moralist ' deprived of all the

pleasures of the senses, exempt from all passions,'
is not the person best qualified to speak of 'temptations' and man's 'lower nature.' Only the
musical can understand the significance of music,
and only the sensual and the passionate can
understand the significance of the senses and
the passions. The sick ascetic can understand
nothing of these things, for the simple reason
that he cannot, or deliberately does not, experience the emotions or perform the acts which he
sets out to criticize. He makes a virtue of necessity and calls his debility by sacred names.
'Those who restrain Desire,' says Blake, 'do so
because theirs is weak enough to be restrained.'
Pascal's sick body was *naturaliter Christianum.*
'Une douleur de tête comme insupportable, une
chaleur d'entrailles et beaucoup d'autres maux,'
would have made it extremely hard for him to
be a pagan. Nietzsche would have been tempted
by the very difficulty of the undertaking to try ;
for Nietzsche held that a sick man had no right
to be an ascetic—it was too easy. Not so Pascal ;
he accepted his sickness, and even persuaded
himself that he was grateful for the headache and
the heat in the entrails. And not only did he
accept sickness for himself ; he even tried to
impose it on other people. He demanded that
every one should think and feel about the world
at large as he did ; he wanted to impose head-
aches, sleeplessness, and dyspepsia, with their
accompanying psychological states, on all.

Those of us, however, who are blessedly free from these diseases will refuse to accept Pascal's neuralgia-metaphysic, just as we refuse to accept the asthma-philosophy of a more recent invalid of genius, Marcel Proust.

## II

### § 11. *Nature of the Normal Universe*

The second section of this essay shall begin where the first ended—with asthma and neuralgia, with heat in the entrails and insupportable pains in the head. Pascal, as we have seen, pronounced himself as contradictorily about sickness as about most other subjects. What he describes as one of the great sources of error is also the Christian's natural state. If he had been asked to reconcile the two pronouncements he would doubtless have replied that what seems error to the normal man, to a member of the 'omnitude,' is not necessarily error in the eyes of God—may, in fact, be the truth. For after all, what is our currently accepted 'reality'? What is 'the normal'? What is 'common sense'? What are the 'laws of thought' and the 'boundaries of the knowable'? They are merely more or less long-established conventions.

Our normal common-sense universe is the product of a particular habit of perception—perhaps a bad habit, who knows? A slight change in the nature of our sense organs would make it unrecognizably unlike its present self. Henri Poincaré has described some of the worlds which such changes in our structure would automatically call into existence. Extremely interesting in this context are certain recent studies of the universes inhabited by the lower animals. The world, for example, in which a sea-urchin has its being is a world, for us, of water, rocks, sand, weeds, and marine animals. For the urchin, however, not one of these things even exists. The universe perceived (which is the same thing as saying ‘ created ’) by its organs of touch is utterly unlike that in which we humans arbitrarily locate it. By modifying the apparatus with which we perceive (and the apparatus with which we perceive is the apparatus with which we create), sickness modifies the universe. For one man to impose his particular universe on another is almost as unjustifiable as it is for a man to impose a human universe on a sea-urchin.

In the course of the last century or two a considerable number of what once were necessities of thought and immutable laws of nature have been shown to be systems arbitrarily fabricated by human beings to serve particular human ends. Thus, God is no longer bound, as he once was, to obey the decrees promulgated by Euclid in 300 B.C. He can now take his choice among a variety of geometries. Geometries and laws of nature are among the latest products of the human spirit ; they have not had time to take root. Such slightly formed habits are relatively easy to break. But there are habits of perception and thought incomparably more ancient, and so deeply ingrained that it seems hardly possible for us to interpret experience except in the terms of them. Thus, the habit of living in space and time is one which was evidently formed by our remotest ancestors. And yet men are now able, if not to live, at least to think in terms of a four-dimensional continuum ; and when they deal with the sub-atomic world of electrons and protons, they must get rid of temporal and spatial notions altogether. The universe of the infinitely little is radically unlike the macroscopic universe which we inhabit. Modern physical theory shows that Pascal was quite right to insist on its strangeness. In the case of time it seems possible for us to *live* in a universe where the ordinary temporal relations do not hold. There is tolerably good evidence to show that the future is in certain circumstances foreseeable (especially in dreams, if we can believe Mr. Dunn, the author of that very interesting book, *An Experiment with Time*). It is quite conceivable that a technique of prevision may in time be perfected, and that the prophetic powers at present, it is to be presumed, latent in the vast majority of individuals will be actualized. In which case our normal universe would be changed out of all recognition.

## § 12. *The Sick Man's Universe : its Justification*

Sickness modifies our perceiving apparatus, and so modifies the universe in which we live. Which is more real, which is nearer to the thing in itself perceived by God—the healthy man's universe or the sick man's ? It is clearly impossible to answer with certainty. The healthy man has the majority on his side. But *vox populi* is not *vox Dei*. For practical, social purposes the normal universe is certainly the most convenient we can inhabit ; but convenience is not a measure of Truth. The healthy man labours under the grave disadvantage of not being disinterested. The world for him is a place to get on in, a place where the fittest to survive survive. Will he, nill he, he sees the utilitarian aspects of things. Sickness transports a man from the battlefield where the struggle for existence is being waged, into a region of biological detachment ; he sees something other than the merely useful. Dostoievsky's Idiot, Prince Mishkin, was an epileptic. Each of his fits was preceded by an apocalyptic mystical experience. Thinkers of the Max Nordau school would ' explain ' the experience in terms of the epilepsy—would explain it away, in fact. But the revelation is not the less credible for being accompanied by the fit ; it is, on the contrary, more credible. For the fit detaches the mind from utilitarian reality and permits it to per-

ceive, or create for itself, another reality, less
superficial and tendencious than the normal utilitarian one of every day. (To be able to see
things in the same disinterested way, with the
eyes of a child, a god, a noble savage, is the
mark and privilege of the artist. The artist is
a man who has revelations without having to
pay for them with epileptic fits.) The Nordauites,
who see everything *sub specie Podsnapitatis* cannot
forgive Mishkin, or for that matter, Shakespeare,
Blake, Beethoven, for seeing them *sub specie
Aeternitatis*. They refuse to admit the validity
of Mishkin's experience. They might as well
refuse to admit the validity of their own sense
impressions. For the mystic or the artist his
revelation is a psychological fact, like colour
or sound. It is given : there is no getting away
from it.

Men of talent may be described as a special
class of chronic invalids. The one-and-a-half
wit is as abnormal as the half-wit, and may as
justifiably, since sanity is only a question of
statistics, be called mad. There is a class of
all-too-normal people who take a peculiar
pleasure in asserting that all great men have
been diseased and lunatic ; it is their way of
venting a natural but not very engaging envy,
of avenging themselves on their superiors for
being so manifestly superior. But even if it
could be proved that these people were right
and that all men of genius were neurotic, or

syphilitic, or tuberculous, it would make not the slightest difference ; Shakespeare may have been the sort of man that a good eugenist would castrate at sight, but that does not prevent him from being the author of *Antony and Cleopatra* and *Macbeth*. The canaille hates its betters for not being like itself. Its yapping can be ignored. All that its arguments amount to is simply this : that the men of talent are different from the Podsnapian canaille and have free access to universes which heredity and habit have closed to the common run of humanity. Illness may facilitate their entry into these non-Podsnapian universes of disinterested contemplation. If it does, then illness is a good. And in any case the acts and works of genius remain what they are, whatever the state of health of their authors. The medical denunciations of the all-too-normal are entirely irrelevant, and would be merely comic if the denouncers were not rendered dangerous by their numbers and influence. It is alarming, for example, to discover that the Eugenists are working to make the world safe for Podsnappery. According to Major Leonard Darwin, the fittest to survive are those who can earn most money. The deserving rich must be encouraged to propagate their kind ; the poor, whatever the cause of their poverty, whether it be illness, eccentricity, too much or too little intelligence, must be discouraged and if necessary sterilized. If Major Darwin gets his way, the world in a few generations will be peopled exclusively by Podsnaps and Babbitts. A consummation, it is obvious, devoutly to be hoped.

Pascal justified his asceticism on theological grounds. Christianity commands us to mortify the flesh and to be without concupiscence for the things of the world. Christianity is divinely inspired. Not to be ascetic is therefore an act of blasphemous rebellion. But asceticism can be justified without invoking the aid of a revelation which no amount of historical evidence can possibly guarantee. It can be justified on purely psychological grounds. Ascetic practices are methods for artificially inducing a kind of mental and physical abnormality or sickness. This sickness modifies the ascetic's perceiving apparatus, and his universe is consequently changed. Certain of his states are so strange that he feels, if he is religious, that he is in direct communication with the deity. (Which, of course, he may be. Or may not. We are not in a position to affirm or deny.) Anyhow, such states are felt by the ascetic to be of the highest value. This is a direct intuition, about which there can be no argument. If the ascetic feels that such states, along with the universe corresponding to them, are valuable, then he is obviously justified in continuing the practices which tend to induce them.

## § 13. *Pascal and Death*

With Pascal, as with all other mystics, ecstasy
was only a very occasional state. So far as we
know, indeed, he had only one experience of
its joys. Only once was he touched with the
divine fires. His daily, his chronic revelation
was of darkness, and the source of that revelation
was not the God of Life ; it was Death.

After a moonless night the dawn is a kind of
decadence. Darkness is limitless and empty ;
light comes, filling the void, peopling infinity
with small irrelevancies, setting bounds to the
indefinite. The deepest, the most utter darkness is death's ; in the dark idea of death we
come as near to a realization of infinity as it is possible for finite beings to come. Pascal early made
the acquaintance of death. Through all the
later years of his brief existence he lived surrounded by the bottomless obscurities of death.
Those metaphysical gulfs which were said to
have accompanied him wherever he went were
openings into the pit of death. All his meditations on the infinities of littleness and greatness, on the infinite distance between body and
mind and the infinitely more infinite distance
between mind and charity, were inspired by
death, were rationalizations of his sense of death.
Death even prompted some of his mathematical
speculations ; for if it is true, in Pascal's words,
that 'même les propositions géométriques de-

viennent sentiments,' the converse is no less
certain. Sentiments are rationalized as geometrical propositions. When Pascal speculated
on the mathematical infinite, he was specu-
lating on that unplumbed darkness with which
death had surrounded him. Pascal's thoughts
become intelligible only on condition that we
look at them against this background of darkness. A man who has realized infinity, not
intellectually, but with his whole being, realized
it in the intimate and terrifying realization of
death, inhabits a different universe from that
which is the home of the man to whom death
and infinity are only names.

## III

### § 14. *The God of Life*

But there is a revelation of life as well as a
revelation of death ; to Pascal that revelation was never vouchsafed. It seemed to him
incredible that men should busy themselves
with their petty affairs, their trivial pleasures,
instead of with the huge and frightful problems of eternity. Himself hemmed in by the
darkness of death, he was astonished that other
people contrived to think of anything else.
This disregard of death and infinity seemed to
him so strange, that he was forced to regard
it as supernatural. ' C'est un appesantisse-

ment de la main de Dieu,' was his conclusion.
And he was right. God does lay his hand on
those who can forget the darkness and death
and infinity—but lays it upon them not in
anger, not as a punishment, as Pascal imagined,
but encouragingly, helpfully. For the God who
forbids men to think incessantly of the infinite
darkness is a God of Life, not of Death, a God
of diversity, not of frozen unity. Pascal hates
the world because it has ' le pouvoir de ne pas
songer à ce qu'il ne veut pas songer.' But the
God of Life demands that men shall live ; and
in order that they may live, they must have
desire ; and in order that they may have
desire, they must live in a world of desirable
things. But ' le fini s'anéantit en présence de
l'infini, et devient un pur néant.' Therefore
finite things must not be kept in contact with
the infinite, because if they were they would
lose their desirability and men would cease to
desire them and so would cease to live. (Pascal's
infinite, it should be noticed, is something external to the finite world. The spirit that
sees infinity in a grain of sand and eternity in
a flower is a life-worshipping spirit, not one
enamoured of death.) Not to desire, not to
live, would be a blasphemy and a rebellion
against the God of Life. So the God of Life
lays his hand upon men and gives them power
not to think the thoughts they do not wish to
have ; he bestows the grace of life upon them

that they may spend their little time on earth, not in trying to discover whether their eternal death-sentence has been passed, 'mais à jouer au piquet.' 'It is supernatural,' cries Pascal ; and we can agree with him. The God of Life is a powerful God ; Pascal knew it, and used all the arts of logic and persuasion to convert men from his worship to that of Death. But in vain. Men still refuse to spend their lives thinking of death, still refuse to contemplate that dark infinite whose enormousness reduces to nothingness all the objects of their finite desires ; they prefer to think of 'dancing, of playing the lute, of singing, of making verses.' Even when their only son has died, they hunt the boar or play fives, or try to make themselves king. Why ? Because life is diverse, because they are not always the same. They think of death when death is near, and of the boar when the boar is near. 'S'il ne s'abaisse pas à cela,' concludes Pascal, the philosopher, 'et veuille toujours être tendu, il n'en sera que plus sot, parce qu'il voudra s'élever au-dessus de l'humanité et il n'est qu'un homme.' In spite of which he demanded that men should raise themselves above humanity—or lower themselves beneath it—by becoming consistently Christians. He wanted them to deny their manifold being ; he demanded that they should impose upon themselves a unity—his unity.

## § 15. *Unity and Diversity*

Now, it is obvious that men must organize their diversity into some kind of singleness. We cannot think successfully of the outside world unless we have some kind of unifying hypothesis as to its nature. (Would it, indeed, be possible to think of the external world as being one as well as diverse, if we had not previously conceived our own inward unity? I doubt it.) If we were without such a unifying hypothesis, if we never constrained ourselves to act the particular part which we have decided is peculiarly ours, social life and purposive action would be impossible. To-day's self would be unable to make any engagement for to-morrow's. As it is, when Tuesday's ego turns out to be different from Monday's, we make an effort to recapture the spirit of the earlier self, we loyally do our best (I speak at least for the conscientious, of whom unhappily I am one) to carry out the programme of thought or action elaborated on Monday, however repugnant it may seem to the Tuesday personage who has to do the carrying out. The task of unification is made easier by the fact that some sort of persistent identity does really underlie the diversities of personality. A collection of habits (among which, if we are good idealists, we must number the body), and a number of hereditary tendencies to form habits, persist as a gradually changing background to the diversities of personality. The colony of our souls is rooted in the stem of a single life. By a process of what Jules de Gaultier has called ' Bovarysm ' (Mme. Bovary, it will be remembered, was a lady who imagined herself other than what she really was) we impose upon ourselves a more or less fictitious personality and do our best consistently to act the imaginary part, whatever may be the real state of our psychology. The reality is often stronger than the imagination ; in spite of all our earnest efforts to bovaryze ourselves into imaginary unity, human life constantly reveals itself as diverse and discontinuous. Pascal demands that all men shall imagine themselves to be ascetic despisers of the world ; they must bovaryze their diversity into a conscious and consistent worship of death. The methods by means of which this bovaryzation is to be accomplished are the methods perfected through long ages of experience by the Catholic church. The external man, the machine, in Pascal's phrase, must perform the gestures of worship and renunciation, until a habit is formed, and the bovaric personage of the other-worldly hater of life is firmly established as an actualized imagination in the mind.

But not every man agrees with Pascal in finding life detestable. For those who love it his world-view and his way of life are a blasphemy and an

ingratitude ; let them therefore be anathema.
What are the alternatives to Pascal's scheme ?
To abandon ourselves completely to our natural
diversity ? Social existence and purposive individual activity would be rendered impossible
by such an abandonment. Besides, we have a
body, we have habits and memories that persist ;
we are conscious of being enduringly alive.
Absolute diversity would be as difficult of achievement as absolute unity. The problem is obviously to discover just how much unifying requires
to be done, and to see that it is done in the interests of life. A life-worshipping personage must
be set up in opposition to the Pascalian worshipper of death, and the diversities of personality
must be unified, so far as it is necessary to unify
them, by being bovaryzed into a resemblance to
this mythical personage.

## § 16. *The Life-Worshipper as Philosopher*

What are the principal features of the life-
worshipper ? I shall answer tentatively and only
for my private personage. In these matters, it
is obvious, no man has a right to speak for any one
except himself and those who happen to resemble
him. My objection to Pascal is not that he wor-
ships death. Every man has as good a right to
his own particular world-view as to his own
particular kidneys. Incidentally there is often,
if we may judge from the case of Carlyle, of

Pascal himself, and how many others, a very intimate connection between a man's viscera and his philosophy. To argue against Carlyle's ' fire-eyed despair ' is futile, because it is to argue against Carlyle's digestion. I admit Carlyle's despair and Pascal's worship of death, just as I admit the shape of their noses and their tastes in art. What I object to is their claim to dictate to the world at large. I refuse to have death-worship imposed on me against my will. And conversely I have no desire to impose my particular brand of life-worship on any one else. In philosophical discussions the Sinaitic manner is ridiculous—as ridiculous as it would be in gastronomical discussions. It is not in terms of ' thus saith the Lord ' that we talk, for example, of lobsters. Not now, at any rate ; for it is worth remembering that Jehovah forbade the Chosen People to eat them—presumably because they divide the hoof but do not chew the cud. We admit that every man has a right in these matters to his own tastes. ' I like lobsters ; you don't. And there's an end of it.' Such is the argument of gastronomers. In time, perhaps, philosophers will learn to treat one another with the same politeness and forbearance. True, I myself was impolite enough just now to anathematize Pascal's philosophy ; but that was simply because he tried to force his opinions upon me. I can be civil to the lovers of semolina pudding so long as they do not want to make me share their peculiar tastes. But if they tried to force semolina down my throat, I should become extremely rude.

Briefly, then, these are my notions of the life-worshipper into whose likeness I myself should be prepared to bovaryze the diversities of my personality. His fundamental assumption is that life on this planet is valuable in itself, without any reference to hypothetical higher worlds, eternities, future existences. 'Is it not better, then, to be alone and love Earth only for its earthly sake?' It is, particularly if you have Blake's gift for seeing eternity in a flower and for 'making the whole creation appear infinite and holy . . . by an improvement of sensual enjoyment.' The life-worshipper's next assumption is that the end of life, if we leave out of account for the moment all the innumerable ends attributed to it by living individuals, is more life, that the purpose of living is to live. God, for the life-worshipper, is of course life, and manifests himself in all vital processes, even those which, from our point of view, are most repulsive and evil. For the life-worshipper perceives, with Kant, that if man had no anti-social tendencies 'an Arcadian life would arise, of perfect harmony and mutual love, such as must suffocate and stifle all talents in their very germs'; and with Lotze that 'our virtue and happiness can only flourish amid an active conflict with wrong.' Following the Hindus, he realizes that perfection is necessarily Nirvana, and that the triumph of good would mean the total annihilation of existence. A homogeneously perfect life is a contradiction in terms. Without contrast and diversity life is inconceivable. Therefore he believes in having as much contrast and diversity as he can get ; for not being a death-worshipper, like the Hindus, he will have nothing to do with a perfection that is annihilation ; and not being illogical, like the Christians, he cannot believe in a perfection that is not a Nirvana of non-existence. It is in Blake's *Marriage of Heaven and Hell* that he finds the best statement of his own life-worshipper's metaphysic.

Without contraries is no progression. Attraction and Repulsion, Reason and Energy, Love and Hate are necessary to Man's Existence.

Man has no Body distinct from his Soul ; for that call'd body is a portion of the Soul discern'd by the Senses, the chief inlets of spirit in this age. Energy is the only life and is from the body. . . . Energy is Eternal Delight.

God alone Acts or is in existing beings or Men.

§ 17. *The Life-Worshipper as Moralist*

Blake is also the life-worshipper's favourite moralist.

He who desires but acts not, breeds pestilence.
    Abstinence sows sand all over
        The ruddy limbs and flaming hair.
    But Desire gratified
        Plants fruits of life and beauty there.

Blake's value as a moralist would be higher if he had taken the trouble to explain how his admirable precepts could be carried out in practice within the bounds of a highly-organized society. The life-worshipper completes Blake's teaching by showing how this may be done. He suggests a compromise which will enable the conscientious citizen of a modern industrialized state to be also a complete man, a creature with desires, passions, instincts, a body as well as a mind and a conscious will. This compromise is based on the recognition and deliberate organization of man's natural diversity. The life-worshipper is not, like Pascal, a man of principle ; he is a man of many principles, living discontinuously. He does not select one single being from his colony of souls, call it his ' true self,' and try to murder all the other selves. Each self, he perceives, has as good a right to exist as all the others. Each one, so long as it is 'there' in possession of his consciousness, is his true self. To those who would object, in the name of the sense of values, to such a conclusion we can reply with a statement of the observable facts. The sense of values is something which persists, is an attribute of the single life in which the personal diversities are rooted. But the values of which we have a sense vary with our varying personality ; what is good in the eyes of one self is bad in the eyes of another self. That which is given is the tendency to evaluate ; the fixed standard of values is something which we arbitrarily impose on ourselves. We take the values of one out of our many personalities and call them absolute, and the values of our other personalities being different are therefore wrong. The life-worshipper cannot accept *a* philosophy and an ethic which are not in accord with the facts of experience. For him each self has the right to exist, the right to its own values. True, he does his best as a matter of practical politics to arrange that the appropriate self shall be there at the appropriate time. The murder of some importunate and momentarily unsuitable soul may sometimes be necessary ; but he will not be a party to Pascal's daily slaughter of innocent selves, his chronic and continuous psychological pogroms. The life-worshipper's aim is to achieve a vital equilibrium, not by drawing in his diversities, not by moderating his exuberances (for Exuberance, in the words of Blake, is Beauty), but by giving them rein one against the other. His is the equilibrium of balanced excesses, the safest perhaps of all (is it not between the far-projecting extremities of a long pole that the tight-rope walker treads his spidery bridge ?). Aristotle was also a preacher of moderation. Contradicting himself (it speaks well for Aristotle that he *could* contradict himself), he also extolled the delights of intellectual excess. But it is by his doctrine of the golden mean that he is best known as a moralist. As a later philosopher remarked of him, he was 'moderate to excess.' The life-worshipper's moderation is excessive in quite a different way. For the Aristotelian adorers of the mean (how aptly named in our ambiguous language !) the last word in human wisdom is to do everything by halves, to live in a perpetual state of compromise. Not for the life-worshipper ; for the life-worshipper knows that nothing of any significance has ever been achieved by a man of moderation and compromise. Aristotle has influenced the world because he was excessively an intellectual, not because he preached and practised the Hellenic equivalent of gentlemanliness. The congenitally mediocre adorers of the mean exist to give stability to a world which might be easily upset by the violent antics of the excessive. Filled with divine madness, the excessive lay furiously about them ; the great Leviathan of mediocre humanity presents its vast, its almost immovably ponderous bottom ; there is a dull and suety thudding ; the boot rebounds. Sometimes, when the kicks have been more than usually violent and well directed, the monster stirs a little. These are the changes which it has been fashionable, for the last hundred years or so, to describe as progress.

§ 18. *Balanced Excess*

The world has been moved, I repeat, only by those who have lived excessively. But this excessive life has been too often, from the point of view of the individual human being, a maimed, imperfect life. Living excessively only in one direction, the world-mover has been reduced from the rank of a complete human being to that of an incarnate function. How sterile, how terrifyingly inadequate as human existences, were the lives, for example, of Newton and Napoleon ! Such men go through life without ever actualizing the greater number of their human potentialities ; they keep all but one, or a very few, of their possible selves permanently smothered. It may be that such sacrifices are necessary and praiseworthy ; it may be that the Genius of the Species demands psychological holocausts from those whom it has chosen to serve its ends. I do not pretend to be in the Genius's confidence. All I know is that a man has a perfect right to murder such of his personalities as he does not like or feel the need of—as good a right as he has, shall we say, to cut off his toes. He has no right, however, to impose his tastes on others, no right to go about saying, like Aunt Jobiska, 'that Pobbles are happier without their toes.' They aren't. He has no right to be a liar or a tyrannical enforcer of his own opinions. Conversely, those who want to live completely, realizing the potentialities of the whole man, have every right to do so without risk of physical or moral bullying from the specialists in one particular excess.

The aim of the life-worshipper is to combine the advantages of balanced moderation and excess. The moderate Aristotelian partially realizes all his potentialities ; the man of excess fully realizes part of his potentialities ; the life-worshipper aims at fully realizing all—at living, fully and excessively living, with every one of his colony of souls. He aspires to balance excess of self-consciousness and intelligence by an excess of intuition, of instinctive and visceral living ; to remedy the ill effects of too much contemplation by those of too much action, too much solitude by too much sociability, too much enjoyment by too much asceticism. He will be by turns excessively passionate and excessively chaste. (For chastity, after all, is the proper, the natural complement of passion. After satisfaction, desire reposes in a cool and lucid sleep. Chastity enforced against desire is unquiet and life-destroying. No less life-destroying are the fulfilments of desires which imagination has artificially stimulated in the teeth of natural indifference. The life-worshipper practises those excesses of abstinence and fulfilment which chance and his unrestrained, unstimulated desire impose upon him.) He will be at times a positivist and at times a mystic ; derisively sceptical and full of faith. He will live light-hearted or earnest and, when the sick Pascalian mood is upon him, correct his frivolities and ambitions with the thought of death. In a word, he will accept each of his selves, as it appears in his consciousness, as his momentarily true self. Each and all he will accept —even the bad, even the mean and suffering, even the death-worshipping and naturally Christian souls. He will accept, he will live the life of each, excessively.

The saints in the life-worshipper's calendar are mostly artists. His ideal of completeness, of moderation in terms of balanced excess, is realized by such men as Burns (about whom the respectable and the academic continue to write in the most nauseating tone of condescension and Pecksniffian forgiveness), as Mozart, as Blake, as Rubens, as Shakespeare, as Tolstoy before he deliberately perverted himself to death-worshipping consistency, as the adorable Chaucer, as Rabelais, as Montaigne. I need not lengthen the list. It contains the names of most of the few human beings for whom it is possible to feel admiration and respect. Those who are not in it are specialists in one exclusive excess. One can admire and respect a Newton, even a Napoleon. But one cannot propose them as models for those who would live well and with all their being.

There have been whole epochs during which the life-worshipper has been the representative man. Our own Renaissance, for example. Looking back, the modern historian finds himself utterly bewildered. Those brilliant and enigmatic personages who move across the Elizabethan scene—Essex, Marlowe, Donne, Elizabeth herself, Shakespeare, Raleigh, and how many others—they seem to him inexplicable beings. How is it possible for men to be at once so subtly refined and so brutal, so sensual and yet so spiritual, such men of action and so much enamoured of contemplation, so religious and so cynical? The modern historian, who is generally a professor, disapprovingly fails to understand. Pledged to a respectable consistency of professional thought and conduct, he is frightened by the spectacle of human beings who dared to be free, to realize all their natural diversity, to be wholly alive. Balanced between their inordinate excesses, they danced along the knide-edge of existence. We watch them enviously.

To the moralist the life-worshipper's doctrines may seem subversively dangerous ; and, in effect, the ' Do what thou wilt ' of Thelema was addressed only to ' men that are free, well-born, well-bred, and conversant in honest companies.' For the others, restraints from without in the shape of policemen, from within in the shape of superstitions, will always be necessary. The best life-worshippers are probably those who have been strictly educated in Christian or bourgeois morality, in the philosophy of common-sense tempered by religion, and have afterwards revolted against their upbringing.

Their balancing-pole is weighted at opposite ends with the good social habits of their education and the anti-social habits of their revolt. For the well-born young aspirant to a cell in Gargantua's abbey I would recommend the most conventional of gentlemanly and Anglican public-school educations, followed, at the university, by an intensive course of theoretical Pyrrhonism and the practice of all Blake's most subversive precepts. The loss of his religious, intellectual, and moral faiths might lead him perhaps to neurasthenia or suicide ; so much the worse for him. But if he were tough enough to survive, he could be confidently left to do what he liked. His public-school traditions would bring him honourably and sensibly through the affairs of social life, while his course of Pyrrhonism would have taught him to disregard the restraints imposed by these traditions on his activities as an individual, or colony of individuals.

## § 19. *Unbalanced Excess*

To those who object that it is impossible to obey Gargantua's commandment without behaving like a pig, ' Speak for yourselves,' is all that one can reply. If one is well-born and well-bred one does not behave like a pig ; one behaves like a human being. In the case, moreover, of a sincere life-worshipper, his religion is a guarantee against swinishness. For swinishness is not a manifestation of life, but a blasphemy against it. Thus, swinish gluttony and swinish drunkenness are devices for lowering vitality, not enhancing it. Swinish promiscuity is not an expression of that spontaneous desire which ' plants fruits of life and beauty ' in the human personality. Your Don Juans love from the head, artificially. They use their imagination to stimulate their desire, a self-conscious, unimpassioned, and so unjustified desire that humiliates, that diminishes, that ' sows sand all over ' those who thus call it into action. Swinish avarice and covetousness limit vitality by canalizing its flow in a narrow and filthy channel. Cruelty, which is occasionally appropriate and necessary and is then life-enhancing, is life-limiting and life-destroying when it turns into a habitual reaction, when it becomes, in a word, swinish cruelty. Indeed, any course of behaviour pursued to the exclusion of all the other possible courses open to a normally diverse personality is obviously, according to our standards, immoral, because it limits and distorts the manifestations of life. In the eyes of the life-worshipper such exclusiveness is a sin. His doctrine of moderation demands that one excess shall be counterbalanced by another. To continue on principle or by force of habit in one course is to destroy that vital equilibrium whose name is virtue, and run into immorality. Pascal, it is obvious, was a horribly immoral man. He sinned against life by a consistent excess of holiness, in precisely the same way as gluttons sin by a consistent excess of greed, misers by avarice, and the lewd by unremitting lechery.

### § 20. *Life and the Routine of Living*

It is worth remarking that the revelation of life confirms many of the revelations of death.[1] The business and the distractions which Pascal hated so much, because they made men forget that they must die, are hateful to the life-worshipper because they prevent men from fully living. Death makes these distractions seem trivial and silly ; but equally so does life. It was from pain and gradually approaching dissolution that Ivan Ilyitch learned to understand the futility of his respectable bourgeois career. If he had ever met a genuinely living man, if he had ever read a book, or looked at a picture, or heard a piece of music by a living artist, he would have learned the same lesson. But Pascal and the later Tolstoy would not permit the revelation to come from life. Their aim was to humiliate men by rolling them in the corruption of the grave, to inflict a defiling punishment on them ; they condemned, not only the distracting, life-destroying futilities with which men fill their

---

[1] I have borrowed the phrase from Shestov. 'La Révélation de la Mort' is the title, in its French translation, of one of his most interesting books.

days, but also the life which those futilities destroyed. The life-worshipper agrees with them in hating the empty fooleries and sordidnesses of average human existence. Incidentally the progress of science and industry has enormously increased the element of foolery and sordidness in human life. The clerk and the taylorized workman leave their imbecile tasks to spend their leisure under the influence of such opiate distractions as are provided by the newspaper, the cinema, the radio ; they are given less and less opportunity to do any active or creative living of their own. Pascal and Tolstoy would have led them from silliness to despair by talking to them of death ; but ' memento vivere ' is the life-worshipper's advice. If people remembered to live, they would abstain from occupations which are mere substitutes for life However, most of them don't want to live, just as they don't want to die ; they are as much afraid of living as of dying. They prefer to go on existing dimly in the semi-coma of mechanized labour and mechanized leisure. Gradually to putrefy is their ideal of felicity. If the life-worshipper objects, it is for his own sake. These people have every right to putrefy if they want to putrefy ; but the trouble is, that they may infect those who don't wish to putrefy. A plague-pit is not the healthiest place to worship life in.

## § 21. *Life and the Future*

When he told his disciples to take no thought for the morrow, Jesus was speaking as a worshipper of life. To pay too much attention to the future is to pay too little to the present—is to pay too little, that is to say, to life ; for life can only be lived in the present. Eternity conceived as existing apart from life is life's enemy ; that was why Pascal laid so much stress on the eternal and infinite. The only eternity known to life is that present eternity of ecstatic timelessness which is the consummation of intense living. Pascal himself reproached men for being ' so imprudent that they wander through times that are not theirs and never think of the only time which belongs to them.' But, as usual, his principles and his physiology would not allow him to practise what his intelligence theoretically perceived to be right. He saw that it was stupid not to live in the only time which belonged to him, but nevertheless persisted in thinking of nothing but approaching death and posthumous futurity. Strangely enough, he seemed to have imagined that his death-worship was true Christianity. But ' let the dead bury their dead ' was what the founder of the religion had said. Jesus had no patience (at that moment, at any rate) with the people who imagine that they have something better to do than to live.

Living too much in and for another time than

the present is the source of other crimes than too much holiness. The undue interest in money derives from too exclusive and excessive a preoccupation with the future in this life, just as undue interest in death and the means of posthumous salvation derives from a preoccupation with the future in another life. Death-dealing holiness is rare in the contemporary West ; but literally millions of men and women pass their time murdering themselves for the sake of their financial position in a worldly future, which the threats of wars and revolutions have rendered so precarious that one is amazed that any one in his senses can waste his time in taking laborious thought for it. The past is as fatal to life as the future. Backward-looking artists who wander in times not their own invariably produce bad works : too much natural piety towards vanished things and people smothers present vitality in the pious. The life-worshipper lives as far as possible in the present—in present time or present eternity.

### § 22. *Habits*

' Two hundred and eighty sovereign goods in Montaigne.' Pascal uses the fact to support his argument in favour of the unique, divinely revealed Sovereign Good proposed to all men by the Catholic Church. ' We burn with desire,' he says, ' to find a fixed framework of reference, an ultimate and constant base.' But we burn in vain. Our unaided efforts result in the discovery only of uncertainty and multiplicity. Therefore, we must accept the divinely revealed doctrines of the Church. It is the appeal to fatigue and fear expressed in the form of an argument. The argument breaks down at several points. To begin with, there is no guarantee that the doctrines of the Church are of divine origin. And in the second place, do *we* (that is to say, all men) 'burn with desire' to find a fixed foundation of belief? All that I know with certainty is that *I* don't burn. And when Pascal says, ' Nous avons une idée de la vérité invincible à tout le pyrrhonisme,' I can only reply, ' Speak for yourself.' The fact is, of course, that these supposedly innate ideas and metaphysical desires are the fruit of habit. Pascal, as usual, understood it all theoretically, but refused to draw the necessary conclusions or to act on his own theory. (Was ever so penetrating an intelligence wedded to so perverse a will?) ' I am very much afraid,' he wrote, ' that this nature is only a first habit, as habit is a second nature.' And again : ' Habit is our nature. A man who has grown accustomed to the Faith believes it and cannot help being afraid of hell. . . . Who can doubt, then, that our souls, being accustomed to see number, space, movement, believe in these things and nothing but these things ? ' ' Our natural principles, what are they but the principles we have made a habit of? . . . A different habit would give us different natural principles ; and if there are certain natural principles which habit cannot efface, there are also anti-natural principles of habit which cannot be effaced either by nature or by a second habit.' Our most ineffaceable habits are those of living in terms of space, time, and cause. But even these, as I have suggested earlier in this essay, can be shaken. Most of our other ' natural principles ' date from a much later period in the mind's history than do these primeval habits of thought. When Pascal says that ' we ' burn with desire to find a fixed foundation of belief, all that he means is that he, together with his friends and his favourite authors, happens to have been brought up in habits of doctrinal fixity. The desire for fixity is not the only metaphysical nostalgia attributed by Pascal to humanity. Men long to know the ' meaning ' of events, to be told the ' answer to the riddle of the universe.' Christianity provides such an answer and satisfies these ' natural ' longings : the fact has been regarded by its apologists as a proof of its divine origin and absolute truth. That Christianity should satisfy these longings will not surprise us when we realize that it was Christianity which first implanted them in the human mind and fixed them there as habits. ' Christian theology ' (I quote from Bury's

*Idea of Progress*) ' constructed a synthesis which
for the first time attempted to give a definite
meaning to the whole course of human events,
a synthesis which represents the past as leading
up to a definite and desirable goal in the future.
Once this belief had been generally adopted
and prevailed for centuries, men might discard
it along with the doctrine of Providence on
which it rested, but they could not be content
to return again to such views as satisfied the
ancients, for whom human history, apprehended
as a whole, was a tale of little meaning. They
must seek for a new synthesis to replace it.'
Why must they seek for a new synthesis? Because
Christianity has established in their minds a
synthesis-habit, because the longing for a synthesis now seems ' natural.' But the ancients,
as Bury shows, were quite happy with a history
that was from the Christian's or the modern
philosopher's point of view quite meaningless.
Their habits were changed and they longed
for meanings. Another change of habit may
easily abolish that longing. In any case, however, the character of the longing does not
affect the nature of the meaning that is longed
for. We have only to observe ourselves and
our fellows to discover that the universe has no
single, pre-established ' meaning ' : its riddle
is not a conundrum with only one correct
answer. Meaning is a notion, like sourness or
beauty.

## § 23. *Summary of the Life-Worshipper's Creed*

The life-worshipper's philosophy is comprehensive. As a manifold and discontinuous being, he is in a position to accept all the partial and apparently contradictory syntheses constructed by other philosophers. He is at one moment a positivist and at another a mystic : now haunted by the thought of death (for the apocalypse of death is one of the incidents of living) and now a Dionysian child of nature ; now a pessimist and now, with a change of lover or liver or even the weather, an exuberant believer that God's in his heaven and all's right with the world. He holds these different beliefs because he is many different people. Each belief is the rationalization of the prevailing mood of one of these persons. There is really no question of any of these philosophies being true or false. The psychological state called joy is no truer than the psychological state called melancholy (it may be more valuable as an aid to social or individual living— but that is another matter). Each is a primary fact of experience. And since one psychological state cannot be truer than another, since all are equally facts, it follows that the rationalization of one state cannot be truer than the rationalization of another. What Hardy says about the universe is no truer than what Meredith says ; if the majority of contemporary readers prefer the world-view expressed in *Tess of the D'Urbervilles* to the optimism which forms the background to *Beauchamp's Career*, that is simply because they happen to live in a very depressing age and consequently suffer from a more or less chronic melancholy. Hardy seems to them truer than Meredith because the philosophy of 'Tess' and 'Jude' is more adequate as a rationalization of their own prevailing mood than the philosophy of Richard Feverel or Beauchamp. What applies to optimism and pessimism applies equally to other trends of philosophical thought. Even the doctrines of 'fixed fate, free will, foreknowledge absolute,' for all the elaborateness of their form, are in substance only expression of emotional and physiological states. One feels free or one feels conditioned. Both feelings are equally facts of experience, so are the facts called 'mystical ecstasy' and 'reasonableness.' Only a man whose life was rich in mystical experiences could have constructed a cosmogony like that of Boehme's ; and the works of Voltaire could have been written only by one whose life was singularly poor in such experiences. People with strongly marked idiosyncrasies of character have their world-view almost forced upon them by their psychology. The only branches of philosophy in regard to which it is permissible to talk of truth and falsehood are logic and the theory of knowledge. For logic and the theory of knowledge are concerned with the necessities and the limitations of thought — that is to say, with mental habits so primordial that it is all but impossible for any human being to break them. When a man commits a paralogism or lays claim to a more than human knowledge of the nature of things, we are justified in saying that he is wrong. I may, for example, admit that all men are mortal and that Socrates is a man, but nevertheless feel impelled to conclude that Socrates is immortal. Am I not as well justified in this opinion as I am in my optimism or pessimism, whichever the case may be? The answer is : no. I may have a personal taste for Socrates's immortality ; but, in the syllogistic circumstances, the taste is so outrageously bad, so universally condemned, that it would be madness to try to justify it. Moreover, I should discover that, if I put my paralogistic theories into practice, I should find myself in serious trouble, not only with other human beings, but even with things. The hero of Dostoievsky's *Notes from Underground* protests against the intolerable tyranny of two and two making four. He prefers that they shall make five, and insists that he has a right to his preference. And no doubt he has a right. But if an express train happens to be passing at a distance of two plus two yards, and he advances four yards and a half under the impression that he will still be eighteen inches on the hither side of destruction, this right of his will not save him from coming to a violent and bloody conclusion.

Scientific thought is true or false because science deals with sense impressions which are, if not identical for all human beings, at least sufficiently similar to make something like universal agreement possible. The difference between a scientific theory and a metaphysical world-view is that the first is a rationalization of psychological experiences which are more or less uniform for all men and for the same man at different times, while the second is a rationalization of experiences which are diverse, occasional, and contradictory. A man may be a pessimistic determinist before lunch and an optimistic believer in the will's freedom after it ; but both before and after his meal he will observe that the colour of the sky is blue, that stones are hard, that the sun gives light and warmth. It is for this reason that there are many philosophies, and only one science.

But even science demands that its votaries shall think, according to circumstances, in a variety of different ways. The mode of thinking which gives valid results when applied to objects of more than a certain size (in other words, to large numbers of objects ; for anything big enough to be perceptible to our senses is built up, apparently, of enormous numbers of almost infinitesi-

mal components) is found to be absolutely in-
applicable to single objects of atomic or sub-
atomic dimensions. About large agglomera-
tions of atoms we can think in terms of 'organized common sense.' But when we come to
consider individual atoms and their minuter
components, common-sense gives results which
do not square with the observed facts. (Nobody, of course, has ever actually observed an
atom or an electron ; but the nature of their
behaviour can be inferred, with more or less
probability, from such happenings on a macroscopical scale as accompany their invisible
activity.) In the sub-atomic world practically
all our necessities of thought become not only
unnecessary but misleading. A description of
this universe reads like a page from Lewis Carroll
or Edward Lear.

Seeing, then, that even sense impressions not
only can but must be rationalized in irrecon-
cilably different ways, according to the class
of object with which they are supposed to be
connected, we need not be troubled or surprised
by the contradictions which we find in the
rationalization of less uniform psychological
experiences. Thus, the almost indefinitely
numerous rationalizations of the aesthetic and
the mystical experiences not only contradict one
another, but agree in contradicting those
rationalizations of sense experience known as
scientific theories. This fact greatly disturbed

our grandfathers, who kept on losing their faith, sacrificing their reason, striking attitudes of stoical despair, and, in general, performing the most extraordinary spiritual antics, because of it. Science is 'true,' they argued ; therefore art and religion, therefore beauty and honour, love and ideals, must be 'false.' 'Reality' has been 'proved' by science to be an affair of space, time, mass, number, and cause ; therefore all that makes life worth living is an 'illusion.' Or else they started from the other end. Art, religion, beauty, love, make life worth living ; therefore science, which disregards the existence of these things, must be false. It is unnecessary for us to take so tragic a view. Science, we have come to realize, takes no cognizance of the things that make life worth living, for the simple reason that beauty, love, and so on, are not measurable quantities, and science deals only with what can be measured. One psychological fact is as good as another. We perceive beauty as immediately as we perceive hardness ; to say that one sensation is illusory and that the other corresponds with reality is a gratuitous piece of presumption.

Answers to the riddle of the universe often have a logical form and are expressed in such a way that they raise questions of epistemology and involve the acceptance or rejection of certain scientific theories. In substance, however, they are simply rationalizations of diverse and equally

valid psychological states, and are therefore
neither true nor false. (Incidentally, similar
states are not necessarily or invariably rationalized in the same way. Mystical experiences
which, in Europe, are explained in terms of a
personal God are interpreted by the Buddhists
in terms of an entirely godless order of things.
Which is the truer rationalization? God, or
not-God, whichever the case may be, knows.)
The life-worshipper who adopts in turn all the
solutions to the cosmic riddle is committing no
crime against logic or the truth. He is simply
admitting the obvious fact that he is a human
being—that is to say, a series of distinct psychological states, a colony of diverse personalities.
Each state demands its appropriate rationalizations ; or, in other words, each personality has
its own philosophies of life. Philosophical consistency had some justification so long as it could
be imagined that the substance of one's world-
view (as opposed to the logical trappings in which
it was clothed and the problems of epistemology
and science connected with it) was uniquely
true. But if we admit, as I think we must, that
one world-view cannot be truer than another,
but that each is the expression in intellectual
terms of some given and undeniable fact of
experience, then consistency loses all philosophical merit. It is pointless to ignore all the
occasions when you feel that the world is good,
for the sake of being consistently a pessimist ;

it is pointless, for the sake of being consistently a positivist, to deny that your body is sometimes tenanted by a person who has mystical experiences. Pessimism is no truer than optimism, nor positivism than mysticism. Philosophically, there is no reason why a man should deny the thoughts of all but one of his potential selves. Each self on occasion exists; each has its feelings about the universe, its cosmic tastes—or, to put it in a different way, each inhabits its own universe. What relation these various private universes bear to the Universe in Itself, if such a thing exists, it is clearly impossible to say. We can believe, if we like, that each of them represents one aspect of the whole. ' In my Father's house are many mansions.' Nature has given to each individual the key to quite a number of these metaphysical mansions. The life-worshipper suggests that man shall make use of all his keys instead of throwing all but one of them away. He admits the fact of vital diversity and makes the best of it. In this he is unlike the general run of thinkers, who are very reluctant to admit diversity, and, if they do confess the fact, deplore it. They find diversity shocking, they desire at all costs to correct it. And even if it came to be universally admitted that no one world-view could possibly be true, these people would continue, none the less, to hold fast to one to the exclusion of all the rest. They would go on worshipping consistency, if not on philosophical, then on moral grounds. Or, in other words, they would practise and demand consistency through fear of inconsistency, through fear of being dangerously free, through fear of life. For morality is always the product of terror ; its chains and strait-waistcoats are fashioned by those who dare not trust others, because they dare not trust themselves, to walk in liberty. By such poor terror-stricken creatures consistency in thought and conduct is prized among the highest virtues. In order to achieve this consistency they reject as untrue, or as immoral or anti-social (it matters not which ; for any stick will serve to beat a dog), all the thoughts which do not harmonize with the particular system they have elected to defend ; they do their best to repress all impulses and desires which cannot be fitted into their scheme of moral behaviour. With what deplorable results !

## § 24. *Pascal, the Death-Worshipper*

The consistent thinker, the consistently moral man, is either a walking mummy or else, if he has not succeeded in stifling all his vitality, a fanatical monomaniac. (By the admirers of consistency the mummies are called 'serene' or 'stoical,' the monomaniacs 'single-minded' —as though single-mindedness were a virtue in a being to whom bountiful nature has given

a multiple mind ! Single-mindedness is all very
well in cows or baboons ; in an animal claim-
ing to belong to the same species as Shakespeare
it is simply disgraceful.)

In spite of all his heroic efforts, Pascal never
succeeded in entirely suppressing the life that
was in him. It was not in his power to turn
himself into a pious automaton. Vitality continued to flow out of him, but through only
one channel. He became a monomaniac,
a man with but one aim — to impose the
death of Christian spirituality on himself and
all his fellows. 'What religion,' he asks, 'will
teach us to cure pride and concupiscence ? ' In
other words, what religion will cure us of living ?
For concupiscence, or desire, is the instrument
of life, and 'the pride of the peacock is the glory
of God ' — not of Pascal's God, of course,
but of the God of Life. Christianity, he concludes, is the only religion which will cure men
of living. Therefore all men must become Christians. Pascal expended all his extraordinary
powers in trying, by persuasion, by argument,
to convert his fellows to consistent death-worship.
It was with the *Provincial Letters* that he opened
the campaign. With what consummate general-
ship ! The casuists were routed with terrific
slaughter. Entranced by that marvellous prose,
we find ourselves even now believing that their
defeat was merited, that Pascal was in the right.
But if we stop our ears to the charmer's music

and consider only the substance of what he
says, we shall realize that the rights were all
on the side of the Jesuits and that Pascal was
using his prodigious talents to make the worse
appear the better cause. The casuists were
often silly and pedantic. But their conception
of morality was, from a life-worshipper's point
of view, entirely sound. Recognizing the diversity of human beings, the infinite variety of
circumstances, they perceived that every case
should be considered on its own merits. Life
was to be tethered, but with an elastic rope ;
it was to be permitted to do a little gambolling.
To Pascal this libertarianism seemed horrible.
There must be no compromise with life ; the
hideous thing must be ruthlessly suppressed.
Men must be bound down by rigid commandments, coffined in categorical imperatives, para-
lysed by the fear of hell and the incessant contemplation of death, buried under mounds of
prohibitions. He said so with such exquisite
felicity of phrase and cadence that people
have gone on imagining, from that day to
this, that he was upholding a noble cause,
when in fact he was fighting for the powers of
darkness.

After the *Letters* came the *Pensées*—the fragmentary materials of what was to have been
a colossal work of Christian apology. Implac-
ably the fight against life continued. ' Admiration spoils everything from childhood onwards.

Oh, isn't he clever! Isn't he good! The children of the Port Royal school, who are not urged on with this spur of envy and glory, sink into indifference.' Pascal must have been delighted. A system of education which resulted in children sinking into 'la nonchalance' was obviously, in his eyes, almost ideal. If the children had quietly withered up into mummies, it would have been absolutely perfect. The man was to be treated to the same deadening influences as the child. It was first to be demonstrated that he lived in a state of hopeless wretchedness. This is a task which Pascal undertook with the greatest satisfaction. All his remarks on the 'misère de l'homme' are magnificent. But what is this misery? When we examine Pascal's arguments we find that man's misery consists in not being something different from a man. In not being simple, consistent, without desires, omniscient and dead, but on the contrary alive and full of concupiscence, uncertain, inconsistent, multiple. But to blame a thing for not being something else is childish. Sheep are not men; but that is no reason for talking about the 'misère du mouton.' Let sheep make the best of their sheepishness and men of their humanity. But Pascal does not want men to make the best of their human life; he wants them to make the worst of it, to throw it away. After depressing them with his remarks about misery, he brings them into paralysing contact with death and infinity ; he demonstrates the nothingness, in the face of this darkness, these immensities, of every thought, action, and desire. To clinch the argument he invokes the Jansenist God, the Christian revelation. If it is man's true nature to be consistent and undesiring, then (such is Pascal's argument) Jansenistic death-worship is a psychological necessity. It is more than a psychological necessity ; death-worship has been made obligatory by the God of Death in person, has been decreed in a revelation which Pascal undertakes to prove indubitably historical.

### § 25. *Pascal's Universe*

The spectacle of so much malignity, so much hatred, is profoundly repulsive. Hate begets hate, and it is difficult not to detest Pascal for his venomous detestation of everything that is beautiful and noble in human existence. It is a detestation, however, which must be tempered with pity. If the man sinned against the Holy Ghost — and surely few men have sinned like Pascal, since few indeed have been endowed with Pascal's extraordinary gifts — it was because he could not help it.

His desires, in Blake's words, were weak enough to be restrained. Feeble, a sick man, he was afraid of life, he dreaded liberty. Acquainted only with the mystical states that are associated with malady and deprivation, this ascetic had never experienced those other, no less significant, states that accompany the fulfilment of desire. For if we admit the significance of the mystical rapture, we must equally admit the significance of the no less prodigious experiences associated with love in all its forms, with the perception of sensuous beauty, with intoxication, with rhythmic movement, with anger, with strife and triumph, with all the positive manifestations of concupiscent life. In the second section of this essay I stated the psychological case for asceticism. Ascetic practices produce a condition of abnormality and so enable the ascetic to get out of the ordinary world into another and, as he feels, more significant and important universe. Anger, the feeling inspired by sensuous beauty, the orgasm of amorous desire, are abnormal states precisely analogous to the state of mystical ecstasy, states which permit the angry man, the aesthete, the lover, to become temporary inhabitants of non-Podsnapian universes which are immediately felt (just as the mystic's universe is immediately felt) to be of peculiar value and significance. Pascal was acquainted with only one abnormal universe—that which the ecstatic mystic briefly inhabits. Of all the rest he had no personal knowledge ; his sickly body did not permit of his approaching them. We condemn easily that which we do not know, and with pleasure that which, like the fox who said the grapes were sour, we cannot enjoy.

To a sickly body Pascal joined an extra-ordinarily powerful analytical intellect. Too acute to be taken in by the gross illusions of rationalism, too subtle to imagine that a home-made abstraction could be a reality, he derided the academic philosophers. He perceived that the basis of reason is unreasonable ; first principles come from 'the heart,' not from the mind. The discovery would have been of the first importance if Pascal had only made it with the right organ. But instead of discovering the heart with the heart, he discovered it with the head. It was abstractly that he rejected abstractions, and with the reason that he discovered unreason. His realism was only theoretical ; he never lived it. His intelligence would not permit him to find satisfaction in the noumena and abstractions of rationalist philosophy. But for fixed noumena and simple unchanging abstractions he none the less longed. He was able to satisfy these longings of an invalid philosopher and at the same time to salve his intellectual conscience by choosing an irrational abstraction to believe in—the God of Christianity. Marooned on that static Rock of Ages, he felt himself safe—safe from the heaving flux of appearances, safe from diversity, safe from the responsibilities of freedom, safe from life. If he had allowed himself to have a heart to understand the heart with, if he had possessed a body with which to understand the body, and instincts and desires capable of interpreting the meaning of instinct and desire, Pascal might have been a life-worshipper instead of a devotee of death. But illness had strangled the life out of his body and made his desires so weak that to resist them was an easy virtue. Against his heart he struggled with all the force of his tense and focussed will. The Moloch of religious principle demanded its sacrifice. Obediently, Pascal performed the rite of harakiri. Moloch, unsatisfied, demanded still more blood. Pascal offered his services ; he would make other people do as he had done. Moloch should be glutted with entrails. All his writings are persuasive invitations to the world to come and commit suicide. It is the triumph of principle and consistency.

## § 26. *Musical Conclusion*

And yet the life-worshipper is also, in his own way, a man of principles and consistency. To live intensely—that is his guiding principle. His diversity is a sign that he consistently tries to live up to his principles ; for the harmony of life—of the single life that persists as a gradually changing unity through time—is a harmony built up of many elements. The unity is mutilated by the suppression of any part of the diversity. A fugue has need of all its voices.

Even in the rich counterpoint of life each separate small melody plays its indispensable part. The diapason closes full in man. In *man*. But Pascal aspired to be more than a man. Among the interlaced melodies of the human counterpoint are love songs and anacreontics, marches and savage dance-rhythms, hymns of hate and loud hilarious chanties. Odious voices in the ears of one who wanted his music to be wholly celestial ! Pascal commanded them to be still and they were silent. Bending towards his life, we listen expectantly for a strain of angelic singing. But across the centuries what harsh and painful sounds come creaking down to us !